PERSONAL
FINANCE
SIMPLIFIED

PERSONAL
FINANCE
SIMPLIFIED

The Step-by-Step Guide
for Smart Money Management

FALL RIVER PRESS

New York

FALL RIVER PRESS

New York

An Imprint of Sterling Publishing Co., Inc.
1166 Avenue of the Americas
New York, NY 10036

ISBN 978-1-4351-6820-6

For information about custom editions, special sales, and premium
and corporate purchases, please contact Sterling Special Sales at
800-805-5489 or specialsales@sterlingpublishing.com.

Manufactured in the United States of America

2 4 6 8 10 9 7 5 3 1

sterlingpublishing.com

Cover design by Igor Satanovsky
Interior design by Susan Livingston

CONTENTS

INTRODUCTION

Taking Charge of Your Finances

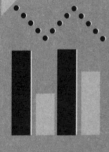

THE NUMBER OF GOALS humans pursue is matched only by the number of humans. Happiness, wealth, success, fame, comfort, philanthropy . . . the list alone could fill this book.

To accomplish those myriad goals, humans use a myriad of tools. Truly talented carpenters can wield a hammer with the same skill that a master painter uses to flick a brush—both blurring the lines between craft and art. Teachers use textbooks, curriculum, and their own creativity to educate the next generation. The best managers use charisma, empathy, and intelligence to direct others, inspiring them to accomplish more than they ever could on their own.

While different people with different goals select different tools, there's one tool that just about everyone uses, with a hugely varied level of expertise. It's something that can help you accomplish any goal you pursue, and it can also pull you away from that goal: Money.

People who see wealth as a goal in and of itself often end up spending a lifetime chasing after it. On the other end of the spectrum are people who consider money useful only as far as it supports their current lifestyle. They will spend it as fast as they make it.

Financial counselor and consumer advocate Dave Ramsey says, "Money flows from those who do not know how to manage it, to those who do." So how should you manage your money?

First, start thinking of it as a tool. A tool is what you make of it. If you own a hammer but use it only to keep papers from blowing off your desk, then you're leaving a lot of the tool's potential untapped.

Most people have perfected the use of tools that pertain to their particular calling, yet nobody can master them all. A skilled accountant can live quite well without ever learning how to use a hammer properly. The accountant might hire a carpenter for house repairs, just as the carpenter might hire the accountant to prepare a tax return. But when it comes to money, nobody can afford to remain passive. Money is the one tool all of us must strive to handle with power and precision. Even the wealthiest person's funds have limits, and what separates the money managers from the money users is the benefit they squeeze from their assets.

It takes no special skill to plunk down $5 for a Big Mac, fries, and coffee. However, even such a mundane task illustrates the importance of managing money. Here are five variations on the simple theme of using a tool ($5) to accomplish a task (purchasing lunch).

1. Anne studies the menu at McDonald's and finds a sandwich she enjoys more for the identical price.

2. Baxter uses a coupon from an independent restaurant trying to drum up business. He manages to buy a better-tasting burger and a larger order of fries for the same $5.

3. Carol pools her $5 with four co-workers, and together they purchase two large pizzas and a two-liter bottle of Pepsi. She enjoys a tasty lunch and brings a couple of slices home to eat tomorrow, ending up with two meals for the price of one.

4. Daniel, knowing he'd spend more than $100 on lunches every month if he purchased the $5 meal every day, instead spends $50 on meat and condiments at the start of every month. Rather than eat out, he prepares his lunches in advance and brings them to work, feasting on variety of sandwiches, including many he can't buy at the fast-food place across the street from the office. And by avoiding convenience foods, he both spends less per lunch and eats healthier meals.

5. Emily decides to subsist on peanut butter sandwiches and ramen noodles for a month. Instead of buying fast-food lunches or cold cuts, she invests $100 in four weeks of cooking classes. The following month, she prepares a mix of hot and cold dishes, bringing multicourse meals to work in plastic containers. Emily now eats as well at work as she would have sitting in her own kitchen. And like Daniel, she does this for less than the $5 per day she used to spend.

All five of these people made use of the $5 tool to improve their lunch outcome. Some put in more work than others, and some used additional tools (creativity, cooperation, education, etc.) to either make the job easier or leverage more benefit out of the original $5. Of course, you don't need to take night classes at cooking school to manage your money. The examples above could have focused on tasks like paying for transportation to work, paying for child care, paying for a vacation, etc. Money can accomplish many things, but only if you manage it.

The following chapters provide strategies for managing money so you can make the most of your resources. Think of these tactics as additional tools to help you wring the most value out of your money.

While the tactics and suggestions to come can help you learn to better manage your money, the most important tool you can draw on to augment the power of money is your own ingenuity and discipline. Remember that money never stops moving. Sure, you can grab a bunch of money and stash it in a savings account, like an eddy off to the side of a river. But the very act of stashing all the money you can actually limits what the money can do.

The true value of money lies in its dynamism—its ability to flow from place to place, turning thoughts into actions and ideas into enterprises—to enrich money *managers* at the expense of money *users*.

Would you like to become a money manager? Good news—you've purchased the right book.

In Part 1, you'll harness the most powerful personal finance tool available.

In Part 2, you'll create a financial plan and discover the keys to managing debt—the most insidious drain on a consumer's resources.

In Part 3, you'll learn how to approach a variety of financial tasks, including investing, buying a home, and planning for retirement.

Keeping Up with the Money

CHAPTER 1
THE BASICS

"Money does not make you happy,
but it quiets the nerves."

— Sean O'Casey

THIS BOOK is designed around three simple premises:

1. You don't have enough money to pay for everything you want.
2. You may not even have enough money to pay for everything you *need*.
3. Your monetary predicament worries you.

These premises resonate because just about everyone in the world faces at least one of the problems.

People sweat money troubles because they feel personal. For too many people, money has become a measure of success.

Ever had these thoughts?

"If I don't make enough to buy a bass boat (or a Mercedes-Benz or a vacation home in Antigua), I've failed."

"If my neighbor buys a bass boat, he's succeeded."

"If my neighbor can afford luxuries that I can't, he's winning."

If any of those sound familiar to you, here's a simple piece of advice that will start you on your way to mastery of your financial situation: Stop the foolishness and grow up.

Yes, it sounds harsh. But if you look at money like tallies on a score-card in some cosmic game, neither this book nor any other book is going to help you. If you look to money for happiness, you'll never find happiness no matter how much you acquire.

Don't waste time crying over the grand dream you can't afford. If you follow the tenets presented in this book, over time you'll either achieve the dream or find one that doesn't exceed your grasp.

Whatever else you do, stop, stop, *stop* trying to keep up with the Joneses, because someone will always have more money than you do. Plus, people with less money than you can acquire more stuff by taking on too much debt or accepting other foolish financial risks—neither of which mean they've won.

Just because Joe down the street takes two weeks of vacation in Belize every year doesn't mean he can afford the trip. And even if he pays for his vacation out of petty cash, it shouldn't affect you. Joe's vacations or Joe's cars or Joe's mansions aren't a problem unless you obsess about why he can afford them and you can't.

WHAT YOU WANT BUT CAN'T AFFORD

When a teenager obsesses over something they can't afford—whether a flashy, fast car or gorgeous designer clothes, or a jet-setting, made-for-TV lifestyle—everyone understands. Who hasn't wanted something beyond their reach? Hormones, ego, greed, and inexperience make a dangerous combination, and luckily most teens are limited—by either their parents or lack of income—on their ability to overspend.

Unfortunately, not everyone grows out of that stage.

FIVE THINGS A LOT OF PEOPLE WANT, BUT ALMOST NOBODY SHOULD BUY

1. A car that costs $50,000 or more.

Between the time you sign the financing papers and the time you settle into the driver's seat clutching a shiny new key, your car has decreased in value about 9%, according to Edmunds.com, a leading automotive website. With this in mind, view a car as either a tool or a toy, but not as an investment. While everyone buys objects that decline in value over time (clothes, paper towels, computers, etc.), few will purchase one more expensive than a car. Unless you drive your car around just to show people what you've bought (stupid) or drag-race (illegal *and* stupid), the difference between a $70,000 car and a $40,000 car just isn't that compelling.

2. A steady diet of restaurant dinners.

If you compare the cost of purchasing food to prepare at home to the cost of eating out, even at low-cost restaurants, you might end up surprised. Say your family eats out only three times a week at $40 a pop. Those burgers add up to more than $6,000 a year, or $60,000 a decade. If a restaurant owner offered you three meals a week for 10 years provided you paid $60,000 up front, would you do it? Probably not. Don't make the mistake of eating up your retirement before you retire.

3. Any electronic device that requires monthly payments.

If you can't afford your new 85-inch TV without borrowing money at 19.5%, then you can't afford it. This rule applies to everyone, no matter how much money they make. Borrowing money to purchase goods that depreciate in value rarely makes financial sense; home electronics lose a lot more than 9% of their retail value overnight.

4. Diamond manicures.

Yes, they exist. Some people pay tens of thousands of dollars to have diamonds studded into their fingernails. Consider this an extravagant representative for a catch-all category—one that includes any luxury item that costs more than a rival product yet provides no added functionality. Think gold toilet seats and gem-encrusted golf clubs. Paying up for quality often makes sense, but once you reach the point where you're adding something to a product without making it work better, it's time to close the wallet.

5. Mutual funds with sales loads.

Every mutual fund charges management fees. If a salesman tells you the fund he's trying to push does not, leave his office immediately, because he's lying. Mutual fund managers expect to get paid for their efforts, and investors always pick up the tab. But sales loads are charges above and beyond the management fee. It's tough to beat the market, and if you include the effects of management fees, most mutual funds don't succeed. Tack on a sales load, and the hurdle gets even higher. For example, if you invest $10,000 in a fund with a 5.75% sales load, the fund skims $575 off the top (hopefully the manager can work miracles with the remaining $9,425). Thousands of funds don't charge sales fees, so before you buy a mutual fund, check it out at Morningstar.com and review the costs.

Don't let anyone else define your financial success for you. Judge your own success solely on your progress on the road toward achieving your goals. If you don't have financial goals, now is the perfect time to set some. And if you do have goals, this book can help you meet them.

In future chapters you'll learn how to navigate the choppy waters of financial planning, banking, borrowing, investing, and how to pay for things you want, as well as things you need.

MAKING IT PERSONAL

To solve your money problems, you must first understand them. For the best view of your money problems, start by looking in the mirror.

Write down your three worst financial issues. In detail.

Yes, it's easy to blow off instructions like this. But if you want to fix the problem, if you want to throw off the weight of financial worry that burdens you, identify the real trouble. If you visit a doctor because you don't feel well, your physician cannot prescribe anything until the problem is diagnosed—and any doctor will not diagnose the problem without considering your symptoms.

The good news is that financial problems are less complicated than medical problems. In most cases, if you don't sugarcoat the symptoms, you can diagnose your own illness. You can't purchase a house because of your $25,000 credit-card debt. You can't pay your bills because you took on a $600-a-month car note on take-home pay of $1,500 a month. You don't have the first clue where your money is going because you don't keep track of how you spend it.

Once you decide to be honest with yourself, you shouldn't have much trouble determining your three worst money problems. But be sure to be more specific than, "I can't pay my bills," or "No bank will lend me money to buy a home."

Here are two better options:

"I put $200 on my credit card to pay bills every month because my income doesn't cover all my expenses," or "The bank says I can't get a mortgage because I have too much debt."

Ouch. It can hurt to write those words. But if they apply to you, then muscle through the pain and record them. Your best chance at finding a specific solution will come after you identify a specific problem. (And don't worry. You won't have to show the paper to anyone. Just fold it in half and tuck it into the pages of this book.)

Now that you've written down the monetary issues plaguing you, here's a dose of good news. Just about all of the most common money problems require the same solution, a three-step plan you don't need an accounting degree—or even a big wad of cash—to follow. We'll talk about the first two steps in this chapter, and we'll talk about the third step in the next chapter.

SOLUTION, STEP 1: PLAN AHEAD

Suppose you decide to take the family on a trip to Yosemite National Park in the spring. Sounds like fun.

If you make no plans until it's time to go, then pile into the car, will you end up with a good vacation?

Doubtful. To pull this off, most people will have to request days off from work, find a place to stay, plan some activities for the family, and acquire any clothing or equipment needed for the trip. And oh, yes, you might need to set aside some money.

While most people wouldn't think about taking a family vacation without planning ahead, far too many will set off on a longer and more complex journey—life—with no financial plan at all.

THREE QUESTIONS TO ASK YOURSELF

When someone says she doesn't know how to achieve her financial goals, she generally means that she doesn't know her financial goals in the first place. Most people are perfectly capable of managing their financial affairs and getting where they wish to go—if they bother to draw themselves a map.

After you ask yourself the following questions, you'll know all you need to set some financial goals.

Question 1: Do I like the way I live?

For this question, look beyond the financial concerns that drove you to buy this book. Consider your career, both what it pays now and your likely potential earnings. But don't stop at the monetary aspects of your work.

While this book focuses on finance, plenty of surveys have shown that money isn't the most important component of job satisfaction. A 2012 survey by the Society for Human Resource Management ranked compensation the third most important factor in job satisfaction, behind both employees' freedom to use their skills and abilities (No. 1), and job security (No. 2). If you can envision yourself working in your current career until retirement, you already know something about both your needs and your resources.

Economists would call the career portion of the question the supply side. Now move on to the demand side. Consider how you live, what you drive, where you spend your time. Do you expect your lifestyle to change in the coming years? If so, will those changes raise or lower your expenses? Also, compare your income to your spending trends. If they match up, then you can probably sort out your financial issues by making small changes. If your resources and your spending diverge now or will diverge later, you may have to take more drastic measures.

Question 2: Where do I see myself in 10 years?

This question sounds like something from a job interview, but employers ask it for a reason. If your goals don't match up with your current life trajectory, an employer may question your ambition, your competence, or both. Now, you may have devised a good answer for the question in a job-interview setting, but in this interview with yourself, don't hedge.

A 23-year-old with an entry-level job at an insurance company who sees himself lying on a tropical beach year-round in 10 years has some maturing to do. On the other hand, a 53-year-old middle manager with a generous retirement plan and a modest lifestyle who sees himself relaxing in his paid-for home and taking regular vacations in 10 years may have a good handle on his situation.

Most people will fall somewhere between the two examples above. Where do you see yourself in 10 years? And where does that put you on the spectrum?

Question 3: Am I willing to make changes to meet my lifestyle goals?

Be careful with this one. Question 3 requires a simple answer—one that will have a huge impact.

If your resources won't cover the cost of your lifestyle over the long term, you have three options.

1. Increase your resources, either by working more or taking steps to boost your earnings potential over time.
2. Reduce your lifestyle demands so your current career path will cover the costs.
3. Borrow to cover the costs.

Of course, a *clever* reader might come up with additional options. Play the lottery. Hope that you inherit money from a rich uncle you've never met. Mooch off family members. You get the idea. Sure, some people might consider these viable options. But only a fool puts his trust in plans that require beating long odds or depending entirely on other people.

In recent years, option three (borrow) has become more popular. As of mid-2013, consumer credit had grown to equal 11.2% of all nonfinancial assets owned by households or nonprofit businesses. In 1988, just a generation ago, consumers held debt equal to just 8.5% of those assets.

American consumers cut back on their debt slightly in 2013, but history suggests such conservatism won't last. The Federal Reserve estimates U.S. consumer debt at $2.97 trillion, or roughly $9,300 for every man, woman, and child in the country.

If you already owe more than your share, why add to the burden? And if you don't, why pick up the burden in the first place?

Option one offers the most flexibility—if you can pull it off. Some hourly employees or freelance workers can up their hours to generate more income. But relatively few individuals can simply decide they want to make more money, then go out and make it. Of course, anyone can improve or update her skills, build a professional network, and seek a better job. However, these strategies take time and effort.

In the long run, boosting your income offers the greatest potential for changing your financial position. But since that probably won't happen right away, most people should turn to option two, cutting back on spending.

Your lifestyle—again, the demand side of the equation—provides you with the cleanest, easiest way to change your financial future. The math is simple. Spend less, and you can keep more of what you bring in.

ASSETS AND DEBTS OF BOTH HOUSEHOLDS AND NONPROFIT ORGANIZATIONS

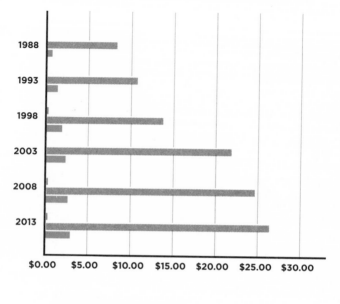

Legend:
- Debt/Assets Ratio
- Household Nonfinancial Assets (Trillions)
- Consumer Credit (Trillions)

Source: Federal Reserve

SOLUTION, STEP 2: REDUCE YOUR SPENDING

Sure, most people like the idea of managing their money, and they really like the idea of having more. Who wouldn't? But eventually it comes time to alter the spending habits, and this is the point at which most people abandon the plan.

Anyone can decide that, yes, he's willing to make some changes. Unfortunately, the path from decision to action can be longer and rockier than it looks from a distance. Because Step 2 is less about reducing your spending than about *deciding* to reduce your spending.

TEN SIMPLE WAYS TO TRIM SPENDING

1. Go generic.

There was a time when the word *generic* carried a stigma, when supermarkets stuck all the generic, non-branded products in their own aisle and didn't market them. Well, those days have disappeared, leaving shoppers with more choices, albeit with less guidance.

When you purchase a famous brand, you pay for the label—and the national advertising campaign. Generic drugs are the clinical equivalent of the better-known name brand, so why pay full price? Off-brand food and clothing might not exactly match the national brand, but you should at least try them out before you dismiss them. Store brands often sell at discounts of at least 25% to big national brands, and in many cases the quality difference is negligible, if it exists at all.

Taste tests conducted by *Consumer Reports* found that in most cases, neither the store brand nor the national brand emerged a clear winner, with test subjects split about which tasted better. Given the price differential between national brands and store brands, the survey represents a definitive victory for the off-brand products.

With many companies now making both their flagship brands and less-expensive products that compete with them, those test results shouldn't surprise anybody.

So try the store-brand beans. If you don't like them, sample another label. And if you decide that the famous brand tastes better, go ahead and buy it. There's nothing wrong with paying for quality—as long as you do it for a reason other than the can having a label with a name you recognize.

2. Avoid bank fees.

This one sounds simple, but the numbers suggest plenty of consumers haven't figured it out yet. According to research firm Moebs Services, banks generated more than $31 billion in revenue from overdraft fees in 2011.

In some cases, consumers with good records for on-time payment can call their banks or credit card companies and get overdraft or late fees waived. It's worth a try. However, by exercising a little more care while paying bills and creating a budget that works, you can eliminate your exposure to bank overdraft fees and credit card late fees entirely.

Automated teller machines (ATMs) will also nickel-and-dime you to death. Actually, they don't just stop at dimes, as plenty of ATMs will set you back more than $3 per transaction if you use a machine outside of your bank's network. Sure, that non-bank ATM is convenient—but using it means you pay convenience-store prices. When possible, just visit the branch. You'll learn more about banking in Chapter 9.

3. Don't fool with pricey fuel.

Even the most respected gasoline companies don't spend a lot of money advertising the benefits of their premium blend. The reason? In most cases, drivers don't reap much benefit from higher-octane fuel, and the gas marketers can't make many claims about their product's superiority.

If you own a car designed to take premium gasoline, you should probably follow the manufacturer's guidelines. Engine repairs can set you back a lot more than you'd pay for high-end gas. But if the owner's manual doesn't advise you to fill your car with premium, don't spend the extra money.

4. Tighten up your taxes.

The Internal Revenue Service acknowledges that millions of Americans overpay their taxes because they miss out on deductions or credits. With today's comprehensive tax software, individuals who understand taxes can do a pretty good job on their own. But preparing tax returns isn't for everyone. If you're not comfortable doing your own taxes but you tackle the job anyway to save a few bucks, pony up for an accountant. If she sniffs out a couple extra deductions, you could reduce your bill enough to cover the accountant's fee and then some. Chapter 9 will provide more tips for saving money on taxes.

5. Use coupons.

These days you don't have to sit down with the Sunday paper and a pair of scissors. Grocery stores still print the coupons, but many also make them available online. Before you shop, visit your store's website and see if you can get 50 cents off that box of Cheerios.

Serious shoppers who live close to multiple supermarkets should consider checking out more than one website. Grocery retailers earn very thin profit margins, and they often compete on price in an effort to boost customer volume. Feel free to play one store off the other, buying milk and eggs on sale at Kroger while taking advantage of coupons for deli meat at the Safeway a few blocks over.

6. Forget the warranty.

According to the Service Contract Industry Council, consumers generally pay 10% to 20% extra to extend a manufacturer's one-year warranty through the fifth year. And a 2012 study by the University of Maryland found 31% of consumers buy extended warranties each year. Most major appliances won't break down before the warranty expires, which limits the value of the coverage. And if you purchase the item with a credit card, you may already have some warranty protection.

7. Pull the plug.

Many modern electronic devices draw current even when turned off, causing a drain on your wallet and a higher electric bill. Because consumers don't need to whip out cash or write an extra check, many absorb this extra cost without noticing. Energy Star estimates that U.S. households waste an average of $100 per year powering devices that aren't being used.

Specialized power strips can cut off the flow of electricity to devices, but for some problems the low-tech solution works best. If you turn it off, think about unplugging it as well. In recent years, chargers for computers and phones have become serial offenders. Have you ever left your phone to charge in the morning, then failed to check on it until late at night? If so, you're only one of millions.

8. Stop supersizing.

This tip applies to more than fast-food meals. If you only watch a dozen of the 200 channels on your cable-TV system or you forget to take advantage of the tire rotation service you purchased with your last set of radials, you've spent more than you should.

Our society emphasizes products with maximum features—and if you use all of the extras in the premium package, you may get a better deal than the consumer who opted for the entry-level offering. But unless you actually tap into all those special features, read the magazines you order from cover to cover, and routinely download the movies or books or whatever-it-is from the subscription service that caught your eye last year, you already know some easy places to trim spending. Features many consumers pay for but don't need include:

- Insurance on rental cars.
- Credit-monitoring services (better to obtain your own credit reports free of charge at AnnualCreditReport.com).
- Automobile undercoating.
- Express shipping. Sure, everyone wants to receive their purchases fast. But if you don't need it immediately, why pay extra to receive it in two days?
- Credit card insurance.

9. Don't pay full retail price.

Careful shoppers spend less than lazy shoppers. With the exception of perishable staples, such as fresh fruits and vegetables, conscientious consumers rarely need to pay the regular sticker price. In an effort to boost traffic in their stores, businesses stage sales. They offer coupons and special holiday deals. They discount to match competitors' prices. If you pay attention to what retailers offer, you can lower your spending on food, clothing, housewares, furniture, and a slew of services.

Don't be afraid to buy used, either. This strategy makes a lot of sense with clothes in particular, especially children's apparel that probably won't fit in a year, anyway. Thrift stores often sell goods at discounts of 50% or even 80% off retail, in many cases for items with very little wear.

10. Shop around.

This strategy walks hand in hand with the idea of not paying full price, but the concept extends far beyond stores.

According to research published in the *Harvard Business Review*, 77% of customers don't want to have relationships with their brands. Brand loyalty has been on the decline for more than a generation. And in the information age, with data about price and quality freely available to any consumer with a computer, you have no excuse for sticking with a bank or telephone carrier or dentist just because you've always used them.

Whenever your phone contract or auto insurance comes up for review, see what competitors have to offer before you re-up. While you're at it, check out other banks and credit-card companies and competitive electricity providers to make sure you aren't paying more than you must. Sometimes your original provider will match a rival's lower price or better service without charging extra, and you win. Sometimes your original provider will tell you to buzz off, and you'll move to a competing company and receive the same or better at a lower cost, and you win. At worst, you'll find out you already have it pretty good. For most people, that qualifies as a win.

Normally, Step 3 would start at this point. But not in this book.

The jump from Step 1, planning ahead, to Step 2, cutting back on spending, requires a lot of desire and a little discipline. But the jump from Step 2 to Step 3, living on a budget, requires a little more desire and a lot more discipline.

To master the art of personal finance, you must approach it like you'd learn any other skill. It doesn't take much effort to study a few basic chords and play the guitar better than someone who never took the time to learn. Of course, if you intend to play well enough so that people want to hear you strum, you'll have to put in a lot more practice.

By now, you probably know enough about personal finance to put you ahead of millions of Americans. But remember, personal finance isn't a competition. Contrary to the popular saying, you don't win by dying with the most toys. Personal finance is the art and science of money management, but it involves a lot more than maximizing your wealth.

While money can't buy happiness, it can smooth out some of the rough patches. More importantly, the ability to live within your means—regardless of the magnitude of those means—gives you less to worry about and makes it easier to cope with life's other problems. Like the guitar dilettante asked to play a full concert, the consumer with a framework of personal finance but not much depth of knowledge and experience will find her skills tested when the situation demands more.

Now you've come to the point when you must choose. Are you a money manager, or a money user?

FIVE RULES OF PERSONAL FINANCE

To become a skilled money manager, there are five rules of personal finance:

1. Make sure you can pay for everything you need before you start spending on wants.

Food is a need; four different types of cheese on your pizza is a want. Transportation is a need; a BMW is a want. Shelter is a need; a 5,000-square-foot home with a pool is a want. Clothing is a need; Armani suits are a want. Entertainment—cable TV, video games, movie rentals, weekly golf games, etc.—is always a want.

You get the point. If you fall behind on your mortgage but manage to pay your cable bill on time every month, you need to straighten out your priorities.

2. Do some research before you buy.

Everyone should know a little Latin, particularly the phrase "caveat emptor," which means "let the buyer beware." Hucksters have operated since before humans used money, and shrewd consumers learn early on that if they don't watch out for their interests, nobody else will. Following these rules requires nothing more than exercising common sense.

- Don't buy something you don't understand.
- If a deal sounds too good to be true, it probably is.
- When someone says the price is only good for the day, don't be afraid to call their bluff. If the price truly is only good today, then the deal probably isn't as good as it looks.
- Never make a major purchase without taking some time—preferably at least a day and a night—to think about it and do some research.

You probably learned these principles by high school, just like everybody else. But for some reason, once people start to earn enough money to buy stuff, they forget all the tips they followed back when they had nothing to spend.

3. Don't make yourself responsible for other people's debts.

Aren't your own obligations enough to shoulder without picking up someone else's burden? While consumers can entangle themselves with other people in a number of ways, probably the simplest and most obvious is co-signing a loan.

Before you put pen to paper, consider why the borrower needs your help. Banks and consumer finance companies want to loan money. After all, that's how they make their own money. While credit regulations have tightened relative to the crazy years before the financial crisis in 2008, people capable of paying back loans—in other words, good risks—can usually still borrow.

In most cases, lenders ask for co-signers because they fear the borrower can't—or won't—repay the loan. When you co-sign, you simply transfer the bank's risk to yourself. Phrased like that, co-signing sounds like a bad business proposition.

Co-signing loans isn't about friendship or compassion or pity. It creates a dangerous business relationship between you, a lender, and someone the lender isn't willing to trust with its money.

When a friend or loved one asks you to co-sign, they put you in a difficult situation. If they do not understand your reluctance to co-sign, it will hurt the relationship. If you do co-sign and your friend doesn't repay the loan, the lender will come after you. And even if you co-sign and the guy fulfills his obligation, neither of you will think of the other in quite the same way going forward.

4. Don't spend money you don't have.

In Chapter 5 and Chapter 6, you'll learn about borrowing, and the difference between good debt and bad debt. Until you understand the nuances of when to borrow and when to tell a lender to keep its money, fall back on the strategy that worked for generations before banks began aggressively marketing debt to consumers: If you can't afford it, don't buy it.

A generation ago, people used to set aside money to save for vacations or cars or down payments on houses. Today, many label that concept quaint or archaic. But remember that consumer debt now equals more than 11% of the nonfinancial assets of households and nonprofit organizations, up from 8.5% just 25 years ago. Back in 1953, another generation earlier, consumer debt equaled just 7% of nonfinancial assets.

Somehow, millions of Americans managed to buy cars and appliances and take trips without borrowing money. The idea may have become less popular in recent years, but it never truly went out of style.

5. Know where every dollar comes from, and where every dollar goes.

Following this last rule requires the use of what sounds like a dirty word to some people: budget.

While the concept of a budget often frightens or angers people, the budgeting process doesn't require advanced math skills, and a budget can become your single most powerful weapon in the fight for financial power. An accurate, flexible budget separates the talker from the doer when it comes to personal finance. Step 3, the last and most important portion of the journey toward keeping up with your money, revolves around the budget.

CHAPTER 2
MONEY MANAGEMENT

"A fool and his money are soon parted."
—English proverb, late 16th century

NONE OF US THINK, live, or spend in quite the same way, so we can't all use the exact same strategy when it comes to digging out of the financial mire. However, everyone reading this book can harness a powerful tool, one flexible enough to work for you, and you alone.

A budget can help you control your expenses. After all, it's pretty difficult to cut back on spending if you don't know where your money is going in the first place.

SOLUTION, STEP 3: MAKE—AND FOLLOW—A BUDGET

Dave Ramsey, known for his presentations on budgeting, warns that if you don't tell your money where to go, you'll wonder where it went. Budgets spring from the simple idea that if you track your spending, you'll gain more control over it. Somehow the household budget has blossomed into a financial boogeyman—something older people fear to discuss with their spouses and younger people shun like an outdated smartphone.

At its core, a budget does nothing more than record your spending choices, allowing you to refer back to them when the time comes to actually deploy the funds. All of us make choices about how to spend our money, but sometimes we forget what we planned earlier, or we lose track of how much we've already spent. And sometimes we just spend the money without thinking about it, fearing what we'd find if we took the time to assess the cumulative effect of our purchasing decisions.

A genuine money manager doesn't fear the truth. She can't afford such fear, because when it comes to personal finance, knowledge truly is power. You probably already know most of what you need to create a budget. So let's start tapping into that knowledge.

If you use Excel or another spreadsheet program, prepare your budget on the computer. But for those of you who prefer pen and paper, any sheet with lines will do.

By way of example, look at the sample budget on page 26. This chart and four others in this chapter will show a sample budget for Jimmy, a 30-year-old warehouse manager who—like you—wants to get his finances under control. Jimmy got promoted last year, and he moved into a nicer apartment. He spends more now than he once did, but since he makes more money, he believes that shouldn't matter. He thinks he's spending wisely, but somehow he can't cover all of his bills, and he bails himself out every month with a credit card. Hopefully this budget will show him where his money is going and how he can reduce spending.

Keep in mind that your budget won't match Jimmy's or anyone else's. After you finish presenting your income and outflows, you'll probably see places where you can cut back, weak spots in your financial wall that you missed only because you never looked closely enough.

Try building your own budget in stages just as Jimmy does.

STAGE 1: THE BASELINE

Start at the top: record your income. Jimmy takes home $4,000 per month, and this becomes his top line. Before he records expenses, he adds two lines beneath take-home pay—investments and tithes to his church.

Of course, investments and tithes are expenses. So why don't they go further down in the budget in the section for expenses? While Jimmy's budget reflects what comes in and what goes out, it also serves a greater purpose—to reflect not only how, but also why he spends. Jimmy sees both tithes and investments as absolute necessities—they are expenditures he will never skip, regardless of what other bills come due. Because those two items are nonnegotiable and will come right off the top whenever he gets paid, Jimmy subtracts them from his income, creating an amount that he truly has the flexibility to budget. We'll call that amount his spendable income.

Be careful with these adjustments to income, and what you consider absolute necessities. Don't use that space for bills, or for any discretionary items. Possible candidates for a line this high in the budget include things like child-support payments or a structured legal settlement—the kind of expenses that can earn you a trip to jail if you neglect them.

Many people, perhaps most, won't even put anything in that space. In these cases, take-home pay is the same as spendable income.

See the next page for Jimmy's budget before cutting expenses.

Now for the painful stuff, because what comes in eventually goes out.

These costs should separate into two categories—regular bills paid every month, and pay-as-you-go living expenses. While you can probably list your bills without doing any research, the living expenses will require a bit more work.

Go through your checkbook and start recording the expenses by category. If you use Quicken or another brand of financial software, you can

JIMMY'S BUDGET: STAGE 1

Income/Expense Category	Monthly Amount
TAKE-HOME PAY	$4,000
INVESTMENTS	$500
TITHES	$500
SPENDABLE INCOME	$3,000

Expenses	Monthly Amount
BILLS	
RENT	$1,000
GAS AND ELECTRIC	$150
TELEPHONE	$50
MOBILE PHONE	$100
WATER AND SEWER	$20
AUTO INSURANCE	$200
CABLE	$100
CAR PAYMENT	$500
CREDIT CARD PAYMENT	$300
LIVING EXPENSES	
GROCERIES	$300
DINING OUT	$200
GASOLINE	$400
CLOTHING	$100
ENTERTAINMENT	$300
MISCELLANEOUS	$100
TOTAL EXPENSES	$3,820
SURPLUS	-$820

use it to calculate an average over the last six months. Alternately, if you can access your account registers online, you can get the information you need to tally what you've spent from your bank's website. If you keep records by hand, the process will take a little longer, but the math isn't difficult.

After you determine what you've spent on different categories in the past, create a budget based on your history. Your categories probably won't match Jimmy's exactly—maybe you don't have a land line or your car is paid off or your rent includes the cost of water. Regardless, create the categories you need and ignore any you don't. Your budget should reflect your personal blend of income and expenses.

Jimmy pays what most Americans would consider normal bills, but right away he spots a problem. Actually, it's pretty hard to miss.

He's spending $820 more every month than he brings in. No wonder his credit card balance keeps growing. At this rate, he'll accrue nearly $10,000 in credit card debt over the course of a year. And that doesn't even take into account car repairs, gifts for his family and friends, doctor visits, or anything unexpected. With his budget in the red, any additional expenses will slide directly onto the credit card.

Not good. Hopefully your own budget looks better. But even if the math tells a scarier story than Jimmy's, don't panic. You just started.

STAGE 2: SEALING UP THE BREACHES

Facing an $820-a-month deficit, Jimmy hurries to the next stage of the budget-building process: identifying places he can cut. For this stage, only a line-by-line analysis will do.

Rent: Given his financial situation, Jimmy probably shouldn't have moved to a more expensive place. But his lease won't run out for six months, so he can't cut here. At least not right away.

FIVE MORE WAYS TO CUT YOUR SPENDING

1. Leave luxuries behind: If you don't need it to survive, it's a luxury. Now, if you simply cut all the fat out of the budget, you may end up inadvertently cutting some of the joy out of life. It's OK to spend money on some frivolous things, as long as you limit your spending and you do it by design. That said, most people can get by with less spending on entertainment and other non-necessities. The tighter your financial straits, the more ruthless you must get with the spending.

2. Refinance: With interest rates well below historical norms, explore refinancing your debt. Can you transfer a high-interest credit card balance to a card with a lower rate? How about refinancing your mortgage? Never stop trying to lower your interest payments.

3. Sell the car: Nobody likes this one, but for many people, the car note represents the second-highest line item in the budget. In early 2013, the average monthly car payment in the U.S. was $460, a hefty

Gas and electric: Jimmy can reduce his costs by unplugging electrical devices and using a lighter touch on the thermostat, but not enough to make a serious dent in his expenses.

Telephone service: Right now, Jimmy has both a land line and a brand-new smartphone with an unlimited texting and data package. If he could, Jimmy would drop the data plan, given his financial troubles, but the smartphone contract will run for a year. However, he can cancel the land line.

sum for most. If you can't afford the payment, sell the car and buy something smaller, older, or both.

4. Ditch the miscellaneous: Any expenditure can fall under the catch-all category of "miscellaneous," which makes spending in this category almost impossible to assess. The solution? Don't classify anything in the miscellaneous category. Break everything out into component categories such as household, transportation, entertainment, etc. Then you can more easily find costs to cut.

5. Scale down the purchases: Put more time into comparison shopping. Yes, everyone is busy these days. But if you're living paycheck to paycheck without setting anything aside for the future— or even worse, living above your means—you can't afford to ignore this budget-cutting strategy. Buy products on sale and switch from name brands to generic brands. And if you're the type who replaces a plastic container when it gets a scratch and purchases new clothes every time the season changes, you'll have an even easier time finding ways to cut back.

Water and sewer: Most people can do little to reduce this bill, and Jimmy is no exception.

Auto insurance: Jimmy has insured his car through the same company since he graduated from high school, and has never once considered making a change. After a half-hour searching the Internet and a quick phone call, he finds a cheaper option.

Cable: After a long day at work, Jimmy loves to relax in front of a good movie. But ever since he prepared his budget, the relaxation hasn't come easy. Jimmy decides to cut the cord, relying on an antenna and an online movie service that costs $20 per month.

Car payment: The payment on Jimmy's new car takes up 17% of his spendable income. In the short term, he can't do anything about this. If he can't come up with enough cuts in other places, he might have to sell his late-model Camry and go with something older.

Credit card payment: $300 covers the minimum payment, plus about $150 on the principal of the loan. Jimmy could cut back here if needed and just pay the minimum, but it makes sense to eliminate debt when possible. So for now, he'll keep sending $300 a month to the credit-card company.

Groceries: In the past, Jimmy has just gone to the closest store and bought whatever he wanted. This week he spends 10 minutes looking at the sales ads in the Sunday papers and another 10 minutes visiting the websites of three local grocery stores. He discovers that by committing 20 minutes a week to looking for discounts, then stopping at all three stores on shopping days, he can trim his food budget more than 25%.

Dining out: Finally, an easy one to analyze. Jimmy commits to taking his girlfriend to dinner only twice a month and bringing sandwiches to work instead of ordering in with the rest of the crew.

Gasoline: Jimmy burns up most of his gas through his long daily commute to work. Not much wiggle room here.

Clothing: Ever since he received his promotion, Jimmy has invested a lot more in his wardrobe. Some of the spending switched his closet over from labor to management attire, but does he really need to spend $100 a month on clothes? He ultimately decides he has enough outfits and commits to spending only on replacements for garments that wear out—as well as the occasional silk shirt or pair of cowboy boots.

Entertainment: This line item surprised Jimmy the most. It's amazing how quickly video rentals, tickets to concerts and college football games, and rounds of bowling can add up. Jimmy's girlfriend, Jenny, also wants to cut back on her expenses. Since more than half of his entertainment budget involved activities with her, the two decide to increase their number of walks by the river and cut back on activities that cost money, at least until Jimmy gets a better handle on his finances.

Miscellaneous: Because he can't figure out how to cut miscellaneous spending, Jimmy breaks it down into categories that show how he actually spent the money. In this case, the categories included household items and gifts, mostly for family members. Jimmy can't cut back much on household items, but his parents have been hounding him about his spending for years. So Jimmy calls up his mom and dad, tells them that he's trying to balance his budget, and that to make ends meet he will not be buying birthday or Christmas gifts this year. They seem surprised, but not upset.

See next page for Jimmy's budget after cutting expenses. After using a couple of short hours of time, a little ingenuity, and a lot of wisdom, Jimmy managed to cut his spending down to match his spendable income. Has he finished the job? Absolutely not. Ideally, he should adjust his spending further to allow for a surplus, plus create an emergency fund. But at least he won't have to use his credit card to cover month-to-month expenses.

Will your budgetary journey follow Jimmy's path? Probably not exactly. The dramatization above was designed in part to entertain, but it also illustrates the *personal* part of personal finance. Because Jimmy's parents wanted to see him sort out his financial problems, they didn't mind foregoing gifts. That might not fly in your family. However, you may have more flexibility than Jimmy when it comes to moving to a cheaper place or cutting back on gasoline spending.

The key to trimming expenses revolves around accomplishing two objectives.

JIMMY'S BUDGET: STAGE 2

Income/Expense Category	Monthly	Strategy for Cutting	New Cost
TAKE-HOME PAY	$4,000		
INVESTMENTS	$500		
TITHES	$500		
SPENDABLE INCOME	$3,000		
Expenses			
BILLS			
RENT	$1,000	NONE	$1,000
GAS AND ELECTRIC	$150	EFFICIENCY	$140
TELEPHONE	$50	ELIMINATE	$0
MOBILE PHONE	$100	NONE YET	$100
WATER AND SEWER	$20	NONE	$20
AUTO INSURANCE	$200	SWITCH COVERAGE	$120
CABLE	$100	ANTENNA/WEB	$20
CAR PAYMENT	$500	NONE YET	$500
CREDIT CARD PAYMENT	$300	NONE	$300
LIVING EXPENSES			
GROCERIES	$300	FINDING DEALS	$220
DINING OUT	$200	CUTTING BACK	$50
GASOLINE	$400	NONE	$400
CLOTHING	$100	CUTTING BACK	$30
ENTERTAINMENT	$300	CUTTING BACK	$50
MISCELLANEOUS			
HOUSEHOLD	$50	NONE	$50
GIFTS	$50	CUTTING BACK	$0
TOTAL EXPENSES	$3,820		$3,000
SURPLUS	-$820		$0

1. **Follow through on the easy stuff.** Some parts of your budget will just scream *cut me*. Make the cuts on paper, then actually reduce your spending. Don't forget the second part of that last sentence—actually reduce your spending—or you've just wasted your time.

2. **Consider breaking with tradition or taking risks.** Jimmy's decision to lose his cable TV and skip gifts for a year illustrates a willingness to make sacrifices in pursuit of a larger goal.

Just about everyone reading this book would probably like to find a definitive list of actions to take. But in real life, personal finance doesn't work that way. Your individual financial constraints require a customized strategy, one only you can ultimately devise.

The bad news is that nobody can tell you exactly where to cut to make ends meet. Jimmy's cuts may not work for you—once again, this is *personal* finance. But perhaps you can sell your car or eliminate your phone's data plan—or even attack the problem from another side and boost your income with some overtime.

The good news is that finding those weak points isn't rocket science. Most of the work lies in making the decision to change and taking the time to make a budget. Once you do that, consider each line item on its own merits and find those cuts.

STAGE 3: MAKING TIME

Once you whip your monthly budget into shape, you will have a much clearer picture of what comes in and what goes out, but finance can become even more personal. Think of the monthly budget as a well-framed photo, but one taken from a distance. Now you must move in for the close-up.

On the surface, your budget may look complete, but it still needs more care. A budget is a living document. It ebbs and flows as money

SEVEN BUDGET CATEGORIES PEOPLE
TEND TO FORGET

1. Auto repair. Cars go to the shop. Even if you purchase models known for their reliability, eventually you'll have to replace the fuel pump or the muffler or the tires. Unless you want every car problem to also become a money problem, insert a line item in your budget for auto repairs. Hold onto that money until you need it. And as surely as spring follows winter, you'll need it.

2. Emergency fund. While experts disagree on the proper amount, everyone needs an emergency fund. Call it a "high winds blow a tree branch through the window," "baby daughter flushes a rattle down the toilet," or "someone falls off your porch and sues, so you need to hire a lawyer" fund. It's NOT a "spa day with the girlfriends" or "I've got to have the new gaming system" fund. Start with $1,000. You'll feel better knowing you have a grand in cash as close as a trip to the bank. Over time, you can build it up until you have enough to cover at least three months of expenses. But jump right on that $1,000, even if it means cutting way back on a few budget items for a couple months.

3. Life insurance. Many life insurance companies charge quarterly premiums. They don't fit neatly into a monthly budget, and as such are easy to exclude from your calculations. In Stage 3 of the budget process, you'll learn how to account for payments made quarterly, or on any other schedule.

4. Medical costs. Sure, you're healthy now. But nobody makes it through life without visiting the doctor occasionally. Ever smash your thumb with a hammer or cut yourself while dicing carrots? Even if you have health insurance, you will probably need funds for a co-pay or a prescription. Set aside a few bucks each pay period to cover medical expenses, and call it an investment in your financial health.

5. Household. This one sounds easy because everyone buys toilet paper, shampoo, and the occasional box of finishing nails. But these costs can add up quickly and skew your budget. Don't fund these purchases out of your food money just because you purchased the items at the grocery store. The household deserves a permanent line item in most budgets.

6. School. Whether you attend school or have kids who do, school costs money. Books, field-trip fees, activity fees—the costs can creep up on you. Because the expenses often don't follow a schedule, it's easy to forget about them. Don't make that mistake. Figure out how much you spent on school costs last year and make sure your budget covers those costs for this year.

7. Kids. This one sounds obvious, but it isn't. Sure, the food your children eat will come from the food budget. Their clothes will be withdrawn from the clothing budget and toiletries will flow neatly from the household budget. But children accrue other expenses that adults don't. Think piano lessons or swimming classes, toys, football pads, and trips to Chuck E. Cheese following a good report card. The possibilities are endless. Either create a line item on the budget for children (perhaps a category for each if you have more than one), or make sure you slot all of their expenses into other categories.

moves, and it changes with time. Knowing how much you bring in for the month and where those funds go can make a huge difference. But unless you get paid monthly and all of your bills arrive at the same time, you need to take the next step.

Start by listing the date when your bills come due. You need this information to keep track of the dollars as they move in and out of your bank account.

For example, Jimmy gets paid twice a month—on the first and the 15th—so he breaks the income and expense components down into manageable chunks. After all, a lot can happen between the time the water and sewer bill come at the start of the month and the time the mobile-phone bill comes at the end. By subdividing the month, Jimmy can pay his bills before they're due and never lose track of how much he can afford to spend at a given time. Check out the chart on the next page to see what Jimmy has done.

To expand your budget, add some columns. List the due date for the monthly bills, then create two new columns for each pay period. The one to the left lists expenses, the one to the right creates a running balance.

For example, let's walk through this process step by step as Jimmy expands his budget.

Based on the date each bill is due, Jimmy allocates the payment out of a paycheck that allows him sufficient time to mail a check to the service provider. Five to six days should do the trick, but only if Jimmy deals with his bills right after he gets paid. If you pay your bills online, you may be able to pay them instantly, or at least quicker than through the mail.

Note that water and sewer and video service—the early monthly bills—come out of the paycheck from the middle of the month. Fortunately, Jimmy has already paid these bills for this month.

JIMMY'S BUDGET: STAGE 3A

Income/Expense Category	Monthly Amount	Date Due	Jan. 1	Jan. 15
BALANCE				
TAKE-HOME PAY	$4,000			
INVESTMENTS	$500			
TITHES	$500			
SPENDABLE INCOME	**$3,000**			
Expenses				
BILLS				
RENT	$1,000	15TH	$1,000	
GAS AND ELECTRIC	$140	8TH	$140	
MOBILE PHONE	$100	27TH		$100
WATER AND SEWER	$20	1ST		$20
AUTO INSURANCE	$120	19TH	$120	
VIDEO SERVICE	$20	3RD		$20
CAR PAYMENT	$500	22ND		$500
CREDIT CARD PAYMENT	$300	21ST		$300
LIVING EXPENSES				
GROCERIES	$220			
DINING OUT	$50			
GASOLINE	$400			
CLOTHING	$30			
ENTERTAINMENT	$50			
HOUSEHOLD	$50			
TOTAL EXPENSES	**$3,000**			

Next, Jimmy records his take-home pay and any adjustments to his income under the payroll date. He will eventually populate columns for every paycheck for the rest of the year. But he's starting small; two checks will do for now.

At the same time, Jimmy records his monthly living expenses, half under each paycheck date. While a half-and-half division works for him, if you tend to spend more on these items at different times of the month, adjust the numbers to suit your needs. For instance, if you make sales calls early in the month and do most of your driving in the first two weeks, you might want to allocate more funds for gasoline from the early paycheck. This is just another example of how budgeting puts the *personal* in personal finance.

Jimmy has $500 in his checking account. He enters it at the top of the right-hand column for the Jan. 1 paycheck in the row marked Balance, as shown in the chart on the next page. Then he builds the column down, adding income and subtracting expenses.

JIMMY'S BUDGET: STAGE 3B

Income/Expense Category	Monthly Amount	Date Due	Jan. 1	Jan. 15
BALANCE				
TAKE-HOME PAY	$4,000		$2,000	$2,000
INVESTMENTS	$500		$250	$250
TITHES	$500		$250	$250
SPENDABLE INCOME	$3,000		$1,500	$1,500
Expenses				
BILLS				
RENT	$1,000	15TH	$1,000	
GAS AND ELECTRIC	$140	8TH	$140	
MOBILE PHONE	$100	27TH		$100
WATER AND SEWER	$20	1ST		$20
AUTO INSURANCE	$120	19TH	$120	
VIDEO SERVICE	$20	3RD		$20
CAR PAYMENT	$500	22ND		$500
CREDIT CARD PAYMENT	$300	21ST		$300
LIVING EXPENSES				
GROCERIES	$220		$110	$110
DINING OUT	$50		$25	$25
GASOLINE	$400		$200	$200
CLOTHING	$30		$15	$15
ENTERTAINMENT	$50		$25	$25
HOUSEHOLD	$50		$25	$25
TOTAL EXPENSES	$3,000			

JIMMY'S BUDGET: STAGE 3C

Income/Expense Category	Monthly Amount	Date Due	Jan. 1		Jan. 15	
BALANCE				$500		$340
TAKE-HOME PAY	$4,000		$2,000	$2,500	$2,000	$2,340
INVESTMENTS	$500		$250	$2,250	$250	$2,090
TITHES	$500		$250	$2,000	$250	$1,840
AVAILABLE TO SPEND	$3,000			$2,000		$1,840
Expenses						
BILLS						
RENT	$1,000	15TH	$1,000	$1,000		$1,840
GAS AND ELECTRIC	$140	8TH	$140	$860		$1,840
MOBILE PHONE	$100	27TH		$860	$100	$1,740
WATER AND SEWER	$20	1ST		$860	$20	$1,720
AUTO INSURANCE	$120	19TH	$120	$740		$1,720
VIDEO SERVICE	$20	3RD		$740	$20	$1,700
CAR PAYMENT	$500	22ND		$740	$500	$1,200
CREDIT CARD PAYMENT	$300	21ST		$740	$300	$900
LIVING EXPENSES						
GROCERIES	$220		$110	$630	$110	$790
DINING OUT	$50		$25	$605	$25	$765
GASOLINE	$400		$200	$405	$200	$565
CLOTHING	$30		$15	$390	$15	$550
ENTERTAINMENT	$50		$25	$365	$25	$525
HOUSEHOLD	$50		$25	$340	$25	$500
TOTAL EXPENSES	$3,000					

This column illustrates Jimmy's purchasing power. As you learned earlier, it won't often match the balance in your account, because you probably have checks outstanding at any given time. The number in the right-hand column shows what the account will contain after the checks clear.

Once Jimmy reached the bottom of the running-balance column for the Jan. 1 pay period—the space to the right of the lowest expense number—he had allocated all of the money from his paycheck and satisfied the obligations for that pay period. He then carried that number to the balance line at the top of the right column for the Jan. 15 pay period and repeated the process.

TIP When creating the running-balance column, don't just add or subtract in rows with numbers in the left-hand column. In a spreadsheet, data entry can become tedious, and you could easily forget to adjust a formula when you make changes. So once you reach the Bills section, just subtract whatever is in the left column from the running balance. If the field in the spreadsheet is empty, the program should treat it as a zero, and the math should work out.

At this point, Jimmy has created a comprehensive, flexible budget for January. To celebrate, Jimmy thinks about ordering pizza and buying himself a new fishing pole. Then he looks at the budget and ultimately decides to make himself a bowl of ice cream.

Sometimes money managers do that. It's called having discipline, and Jimmy doesn't have much choice because his budget doesn't leave any slack. Every dime of his income is spent before he brings it home.

After the last expense from the second paycheck, he has $500 left, the same amount he started with. Since Jimmy's monthly income perfectly matches his expenses, starting and ending at the same place means he did it right.

Odds are, you'll start out with either a surplus or a deficit, so don't worry if your budget doesn't circle back around as neatly as Jimmy's. Frankly, you shouldn't worry much about how your budget's math works yet.

In Chapter 3 you'll learn how to perfect your budget, including how to ensure that the budget you whipped up actually works once there's money riding on it. Right now, the important factor is that you have a budget. Revel in that accomplishment and take pride in the knowledge that you've begun to make finance personal.

Ready for more? Then turn to the next chapter, and see how Jimmy adapted when life threw him a curveball.

CHAPTER 3
HOW NOT TO BUST THE BUDGET

"A simple fact that is hard to learn is that the time to save money is when you have some."

— Joe Moore

YOU CAN'T FAULT JIMMY for feeling pretty good about himself. He made the decision to change his spending habits, then created a budget that will help him better track that spending. But just when Jimmy thought he had sorted out his budget, his situation changed. He proposed to Jenny, and she said yes.

Jimmy, fresh off his budget-building success, decides not to make the mistake of spending more time planning for a wedding than planning for his life with Jenny. When he attempts to revise the budget, he learns that marriage adds a few wrinkles to the process:

- Jenny gets paid every two weeks, so her paychecks don't come at the same time as Jimmy's. Her first paycheck in January arrives on the fifth.
- Jenny's lifestyle requires accounting for a few expense categories Jimmy didn't need.
- They plan to buy a house as soon as they get married.
- Jenny drives an ancient Honda Civic. It's paid off, but after 250,000 miles it spends more time in the shop than it once did.

Jimmy needs to revamp the budget to account for his new life with Jenny. She works in a department store and doesn't make as much as Jimmy, but two incomes make for a huge difference in a budget. While they won't actually merge their finances for a few months, he prepares a joint budget as a starter.

Jenny brings home $1,200 every two weeks for 26 pay periods in the year, which averages out to $2,600 per month. While her addition to the household does boost expenses, it's not by so much that the extra income is offset. With two paying the bills, the budget now runs at a surplus.

The couple's combined budget started January with $500 in the bank. After taking into account all of the expected income and costs, they should end the month with $860.

Let's take a look at their new budget below.

Some of the budget changes require additional explanation:

Income. The budget should usually revolve around the largest salary. Since Jimmy makes more, his pay periods remain the key dates. Jenny's

BUDGET FOR JIMMY AND JENNY

Income/Expense Category	Monthly Amount	Date Due	June 1		June 15	
BALANCE				$500		$295
JIMMY'S TAKE-HOME PAY	$4,000		$2,000	$2,500	$2,000	$2,295
JENNY'S TAKE-HOME PAY	$2,600		$1,200	$3,700	$1,200	$3,495
INVESTMENTS	$800		$400	$3,300	$400	$3,095
TITHES	$800		$400	$2,900	$400	$2,695
AVAILABLE TO SPEND	$5,000			$2,900		$2,695

Expenses						
BILLS						
MORTGAGE	$1,300	15TH	$1,300	$1,600		$2,695
GAS AND ELECTRIC	$200	8TH	$200	$1,400		$2,695
MOBILE PHONE	$150	27TH		$1,400	$150	$2,545
WATER AND SEWER	$40	1ST		$1,400	$40	$2,505
AUTO INSURANCE	$200	19TH	$200	$1,200		$2,505
VIDEO SERVICE	$20	3RD		$1,200	$20	$2,485
CAR PAYMENT	$500	22ND		$1,200	$500	$1,985
CREDIT CARD PAYMENT	$300	21ST		$1,200	$300	$1,685
SECOND CREDIT CARD	$140	6TH	$140	$1,060		$1,685
GYM MEMBERSHIP	$60	25TH		$1,060	$60	$1,625
LIVING EXPENSES						
GROCERIES	$350		$175	$885	$175	$1,450
DINING OUT	$150		$75	$810	$75	$1,375
GASOLINE	$500		$250	$560	$250	$1,125
CLOTHING	$100		$50	$510	$50	$1,075
ENTERTAINMENT	$100		$50	$460	$50	$1,025
HOUSEHOLD	$60		$30	$430	$30	$995
HAIR STYLING	$50		$25	$405	$25	$970
PRESCRIPTIONS	$60		$30	$375	$30	$940
AUTO REPAIR	$100		$50	$325	$50	$890
PUBLICATIONS	$60		$30	$295	$30	$860
TOTAL EXPENSES	$4,440					

Jan. 5 paycheck slots into the first set of columns. Her next check, Jan. 19, will fit into the second set of columns. Because Jenny gets paid more often than Jimmy, a couple times a year she'll receive two paychecks during one of Jimmy's pay periods.

Adjustments to income. Jimmy boosts spending on tithes and investments to accommodate Jenny's salary.

Bills. Most of the bills will rise. The house will cost more than the apartment, and the couple must pay for two mobile phones and insure two cars. Jimmy must also account for Jenny's credit card and gym membership.

Living expenses. Here Jimmy must estimate. As he and Jenny figure out what they really spend on food, gasoline, etc., he'll adjust the allocations. Jenny also adds some expenses to this section. She visits a hair stylist once a month and takes two maintenance prescriptions for chronic illnesses. By allocating $100 per month for auto repairs, Jenny can set aside a few bucks to pay her cousin to replace the Civic's parts when they wear out. In addition, Jenny reads constantly. To cover the cost of her newspaper and magazine subscriptions and frequent online book purchases, Jimmy sets up a Publications category.

The changes Jimmy made won't apply to your budget directly. But the process he used to adapt his budget to new realities provides a blueprint anyone can use. So how does your budget stack up?

Hopefully you managed to reduce your expenses to the point that you bring in more than you spend. But even if your budget is tight, knowing where the money goes should eliminate some of the uncertainty and ease some of the worry. Even if creating the budget reveals problems—like a lifestyle you can't afford but also can't slim down quickly—at least you'll know what the problems are. You can't fight what you can't see. But once you set up a budget that accurately tracks your financial footprints, the problem areas tend to stick out.

If your budget yields a surplus, start thinking about where to put it. Consumer debt—particularly credit card debt or accounts at retail stores—should vault near the top of the list. You'll hear a lot more about debt—and how to get out of it—in Chapters 5 and 6.

TOP 5 USES FOR EXTRA MONEY

So you have a surplus. Good job. Now you can put it to work. Below you'll find five good places to deploy the money left at the end of the month, in order of importance.

1. Emergency fund. Before you fund anything else, set aside at least $1,000 for emergencies. Whenever you dip into that emergency fund, replacing that money jumps back to priority one.

2. Debt payoff. Life without debt beats life with debt. Enough said.

3. Savings and investment. You're never too young to start putting money aside for the future. And you're never too old, either.

4. Major purchases. You know you want that new couch in the front window of the furniture store. You can almost smell the leather when you drive past. Of course, you don't want to charge the $1,500 sofa. But if you set aside $300 a month, you can waltz right in and pay cash for it in about five months.

5. Higher allocations. If you created your budget right, you set aside just enough to cover your typical spending on food, gasoline, etc. But not every month plays out the same way. After living by the budget for a few months, you'll know which category could use some extra funding. Once you work your way into a surplus, it's OK to boost the allocation in a couple of categories. Just don't go overboard, or you might end up back where you started.

ADVANCED BUDGETING

Don't let the headline fool you. This isn't budgeting for MBAs, just the next logical step for any money manager who has created a paycheck-by-paycheck budget.

Anybody can come up with arguments against credit cards. They allow you to run up debt, they charge too much interest, and they can trash your credit rating if you're not careful. Debit cards don't inspire that kind of passion. In fact, debit cards make a lot of sense. They allow you to access funds in your checking account rather than borrow from a bank. No debt, no interest, no problem, right?

Well, yes, there is a problem. A study published in the *Journal of Consumer Research* in 2011 found that consumers using credit or debit cards tend to focus on the benefits of the purchase, while those who must fork over cash think more about the cost. Something about the feel of money changing hands makes people think twice about impulse purchases, and something about using plastic seems to insulate consumers from the fact that they are actually spending money when they swipe that card.

Research suggests the problem isn't as bad with debit cards as it is with credit cards, but according to consumer advocate Dave Ramsey and others, people still tend to spend more with debit cards than they would with cash alone.

Does this mean you should cut up all your cards? With credit cards, the answer is probably yes (more on that in Chapter 6), but you should hold onto your debit card. Just don't use it all the time.

Paying for goods and services with cash will help you live within your budget. While allocating $150 for food from your current paycheck is one thing, keeping track of that $150 to avoid overspending is something else entirely. Suppose you withdraw three fifties from the bank after you get paid and store them in an envelope marked "food." When shopping day

FIVE TIPS FOR MANAGING A BUDGET

Magazine publisher and author William Feather warned, "A budget tells us what we can't afford, but it doesn't keep us from buying it."

Feather had a point. Only you can prevent financial fires. And now that you know how to budget, you no longer have an excuse for allowing preventable fires.

However, you won't be able to avoid every financial problem. In addition, you probably made some mistakes in your first budget that will require correction later. With that in mind, here are five tips for managing your budget.

1. Understand that it won't work at first. You almost certainly underfunded some categories, and you may have overfunded others. After a month or two or three, you'll have a better handle on what you require.

2. Adjust the budget as needed. Situations change. You could get a raise, or your home may need new siding. Or, after a few months using the budget, you realize that if you don't start picking up a pizza on Fridays you'll go crazy. No line item on the budget is sacred. If you wish to allocate more to a category, go ahead. But make sure you offset it with a decrease somewhere else.

3. Find a place for windfalls. Sometimes money seems to fall out of the sky. A refund check, a gift, a legal settlement, etc. When you receive a windfall, you may feel a temptation to simply boost the entertainment budget for this pay period. Resist it. Go ahead and blow a little of the money if you like—after all, it's *your* money—but allocate the bulk of it for investment or debt payoff or something else that will contribute to your overall financial health. Whatever >>

you do, don't count on a one-time infusion of cash to cover a short-fall in a recurring expense over the long term. If you add some money to the general budget for a month or two to make up the deficit, you delay problems but don't solve them.

4. Stick with it. Sometimes you won't like what the budget tells you, especially when unexpected expenses hit. Cars fail to start, arms get broken, and strangely enough, Christmas comes on Dec. 25 this year. Yes, that last one was a joke, but way too many people seem surprised when they discover that they can't pay for Christmas presents. Good money managers start thinking about Christmas in the spring and set aside money in smaller chunks. Then, when it's time to shop, you can hit the stores armed with enough cash to make all of your gift recipients merry, without putting any extra strain on your budget.

5. Roll with the changes. You must build flexibility into your budget, but more importantly, build it into yourself as well. As Charles Swindoll wrote, "I am convinced that life is 10% what happens to me and 90% how I react to it." Only the adaptable survive.

rolls around, you grab a couple of those fifties and run to the store. After a few shopping trips, when the envelope holds nothing but a five-dollar bill and a few dimes, you know you've spent your allocation, and that you should live on what's left in the fridge until payday.

Start small by using cash for food and gasoline. Once you get used to it, consider going to cash with more of your living expenses.

PERFORM REGULAR MAINTENANCE

Think of your new budget like a new car. Sure, it runs well and doesn't show any signs of strain at first. However, if you don't maintain your car—if you don't change the oil and rotate the tires—eventually you'll run into problems.

Budgets suffer the same deterioration, except those problems manifest themselves earlier. Fortunately, budget maintenance takes little time and costs you nothing. In fact, dealing with problems as they occur—and preferably *before* they occur—can save you boatloads of money.

Once per pay period, preferably a day or two before your next check, compare your checkbook register to your budget. If you see a discrepancy—generally if the checkbook shows a lower balance than the budget says it should—find out why. Did you buy an extra meal out with the debit card? Was it that battery you bought when the car wouldn't start? No, it was definitely the emergency overnight trip to visit your sick mother. Again, it's important to always know where your money goes.

If you spent more than you planned or have incurred expenses you didn't expect, don't panic. Just report these extra expenses on the budget. For example: Suppose Jimmy took Jenny out for dinner twice during the first half of the month and spent his entire monthly allotment of $50. He could change the expense entry in the first set of columns to $50, then change the matching expense entry in the second set of columns to $0. The change reflects Jimmy's spending of some money earlier than budgeted, and it allows Jimmy to stay on budget for the month—as long as he lives by the new number and doesn't go out to eat during the second half of the month.

Remember, the budget can tell you how to spend your money based on the plans and limitations you set up yourself, but only you can make the decision to live by the budget. The budget is your guide, not your boss.

ADD SOME ROWS

You've already built a budget that accurately reflects the money you normally earn and normally spend. But no budget is bulletproof, and none of us live an entirely normal life. Things change, and you should be able to adapt when they do.

At the bottom of your budget, add a few rows with no labels or amounts. Extend the column with the running balance down through those rows, providing space to address unexpected expenses that don't fit in a particular column.

Suppose your son requests extra money to travel to a regional competition with the school band, or your daughter joins the softball team and needs some equipment. Just add the expenses to the budget and the balance will adjust. If you find yourself using these rows often, you've probably discovered a category that deserves its own row in the budget.

Over time, your budget will change. You'll add and subtract rows as you pay off your car or buy a home. You'll add rows for vacation savings or auto repairs or school expenses. This doesn't mean your budget failed or you made a mistake earlier. It just means your budget is growing with you.

LOOK AHEAD

Now that you've budgeted for two consecutive paychecks, try extending your budget further out. Start with three months, then work your way up to a year. Just create more columns, two for each pay period, and follow the steps presented earlier. By doing this, you greatly increase the flexibility of your budget. Here's how:

- When you have six months of income and expenses mapped out, you can easily deal with expenses and income that come up less frequently than your main paycheck. Suppose you receive a

TEN ITEMS YOU SHOULD CONSIDER BUYING USED

You can find used items at flea markets, thrift stores, or consignment shops, with the last two outlets best known for their clothes. Bargain shoppers may also want to check out garage sales or websites such as Craigslist and eBay.

Here's a list of items you might want to buy used rather than new:

1. Tools. Hand tools like hammers, wrenches, shovels, and screwdrivers can last for years.

2. Tablet computers and smartphones. Many manufacturers or retailers will refurbish items returned by customers. If you find a refurbished device that sells for half the price of a new item, you may have a winner.

3. Playground equipment and bicycles. Anything that children use, particularly outdoors, will be outgrown or become worn before too long, limiting the benefit of buying new. Parents frequently sell these items at prices way below their original cost after their children outgrow them.

4. Furniture. After the kids spend a few months taking meals at that shiny kitchen table, it won't look new anymore. Is six months of shine worth the $400 you might save buying used?

5. Baby gear. Strollers, cribs, high chairs, mechanical swings, and changing tables are necessities during the kids' early years. But as they age, these items just take up space. Just make sure to check for safety recalls before you buy, starting at www.recalls.gov. >>

6. Designer clothing. If you're the type who enjoys $300 suits, $200 dresses, and $100 jeans, visit an upscale consignment shop. A $20 item can only be discounted so much, but high-end garments—often donated by picky shoppers who wear the items only a few times—may require massive markdowns before bargains shoppers will show any interest. Sometimes you'll even find new items, complete with tags.

7. Exercise equipment. Everyone knows people like this. They pledge to get fit, purchasing a treadmill or stair-stepper, then lose interest. After a while, they get tired of using the thing as a clothes hanger and decide to sell it. Shoppers can frequently find high-priced equipment in great condition selling well below retail.

8. Lawn equipment. How often do you pull out your leaf blower or edger or chainsaw? Unless you know a lot about engines, you can't count on used equipment to last as long as new. But consider the price per use. Suppose you pay $250 for a chainsaw that you use about twice a year for five years before it breaks down or gets damaged. In effect you've rented it at $25 a pop. You might be better off paying $50 for a used model. If you get just three uses out of it, you've come out ahead.

9. Books. Cost-sensitive readers can find paperbacks for 50 cents or less at library book drives, used-book stores, or yard sales. The fact that someone read the book before you won't reduce your enjoyment of the story.

10. Video games. With national chains like GameStop, Best Buy, and Walmart now selling used games, you can blast more aliens for your buck than ever before.

quarterly bonus check. You can add a row to the income portion of the budget, then enter a balance for the bonus on the date you receive it. The rest of the numbers will adjust.

- Periodically scrolling down the budget to three months, six months, or even a year ahead of the current date can help you spot trends. Sometimes a budget looks fine from week to week, but six months down the road your expenses will have gobbled up your entire surplus. You could also find the opposite—that you're building up more money than expected—which puts you in the enviable position of figuring out how to spend the surplus. (Hint: Saving and investing are always good options.)

- Having all the numbers before you makes it easy to test new possibilities. Say you decide in February to spend $500 on Christmas gifts, but you don't have the cash now. See what happens if you add a row for gifts and set aside $50 a month. Can you save up enough for a cheery Christmas without sending the budget into the red? If not, where can you cut back to make it happen?

If you've followed the steps presented in the previous paragraphs, congratulations. By creating a budget, you've already joined the elite. Gallup's 2013 Economy and Personal Finance survey revealed that only 32% of Americans prepare a detailed monthly budget. Even among Americans with college degrees, fewer than 40% use a budget.

Of course, creating the budget won't help if you fail to live by it. Even if the Gallup survey had asked people whether they actually relied on the budget to drive their spending decisions, you couldn't trust the answer. But it's safe to assume that the percentage of Americans who live within their written budget every month is well below 32%.

PART 2

Building the Financial House

CHAPTER 4

MAKING YOUR
FINANCIAL PLAN

"When I was young I thought that money
was the most important thing in life;
now that I am old I know that it is."
—Oscar Wilde

IT REQUIRES COURAGE to take the leap and decide to put your financial house in order. It takes desire to decide to reduce your spending, and it requires discipline to fashion a budget. A true money manager needs a healthy dose of all three attributes. If a budget that effectively identifies your income and expenses now sits in front of you—particularly if it yields a surplus each month—then you've proven to yourself that you have what it takes. Congratulations. You've achieved the first major milestone in the journey toward personal financial freedom. This accomplishment probably won't excite your friends and neighbors, and you probably won't find a cheering section waiting for you at home. But remember, you're pursuing *personal* finance. Brandish your budget with pride and take the next step.

The journey is far from over, and plenty of obstacles remain. Fortunately, you are now better prepared. Think of your budget and the skills you've picked up in Part 1 of this book as a money-managing toolbox. Armed with the proper tools, a money manager can tackle pretty much any financial project. Still, anyone who owns a well-stocked toolbox can attest that some tools require more skill and practice than others. Anyone can turn a screwdriver, but fewer people can make full use of a miter saw or a soldering torch without practice, instruction, or both.

Part 2 of this book will teach you how to make the most of the tools you have, and introduce a few others. Next up: planning for the future.

THE POWER OF TIME

Your budget can help you take control of your finances in the near term. Since nobody can accurately chart a course for the financial future while still wrestling with the pressure of covering week-to-week costs, starting with the short-term budget makes sense. But now you've got the budget. And while you'll probably need at least a couple months to analyze your cash flow and finalize all the budget items, you can now start thinking ahead.

It's never too late to start carving out a financial future. However, both common sense and mathematics tell us that the earlier you begin, the better. The charts on the next pages illustrate this point. If you can set aside $250 per month out of your budget, in 10 years the savings will have grown to $30,000. It doesn't take complex math to determine that saving for 20 years will double that amount, 30 years will triple it, and 40 years will quadruple it, leaving you with $120,000.

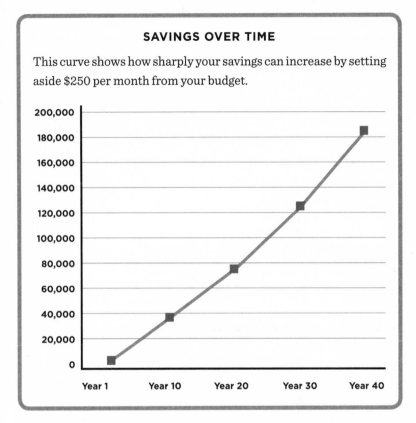

SAVINGS OVER TIME

This curve shows how sharply your savings can increase by setting aside $250 per month from your budget.

But the true power of time lies in compounding. After all, you won't just hide this money under your mattress. If you save the money, it can earn interest. If you invest the money, it can earn interest or dividends, as well as increase in value (more on investing in Chapter 7).

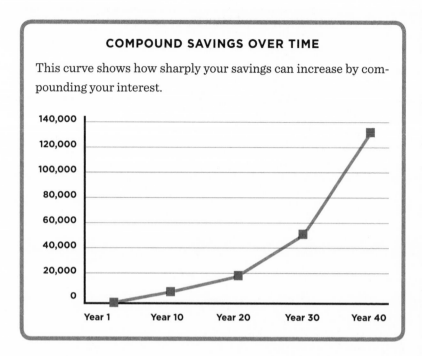

COMPOUND SAVINGS OVER TIME

This curve shows how sharply your savings can increase by compounding your interest.

For example, suppose you keep the funds in a savings account, earning an average of 2% a year over the long haul. In 10 years, instead of having just $30,000 buried in the ground behind your house, you'd have $32,849 in the bank. That's an extra $2,849—or 9.5% more than you'd have if you didn't earn any interest. If you saved for 40 years? You'd have $181,206—or nearly 51% more than you'd accumulate by just keeping the money in a shoebox. The extra $61,206 from 40 years of savings is well more than four times the 10-year total of $2,849, and you can credit compounding for the surplus.

How does it work? Start with $1,000. If you earn 10% annually on that $1,000, at the end of the first year it's worth $1,100. Reinvest that $1,100 at 10% again, and you finish the second year with $1,210, earning

$100 on the original $1,000 and $10 on the $100 you earned last year. At first, $10 doesn't sound like much. But over time, the new earnings on old earnings add up. The longer you can keep building the nest egg before you need it, the more compounding grows the balance.

The numbers really get impressive when you boost the return above 2% for a savings account. Invest at 6% a year, probably in a combination of stock and bond mutual funds, and your investment of $250 per month ($3,000 per year) will grow to $39,542 in 10 years, an increase of more than 30%.

START SAVING NOW

The benefits of saving while young are both obvious and massive, yet most young people pass up those benefits. A 2011 survey by the brokerage firm found that 55% of Generation Y hadn't yet started saving for retirement, while 64% didn't even think about it. Additionally,

- Nearly three-quarters of Generation Y'ers think they're not saving enough for retirement.
- In the 2012 survey, fears that Social Security will run out of money had 40% of Generation Y'ers worried they'll have to work during retirement—well above the 27% who felt that way three years earlier, in the midst of the recession.
- The average Gen Y respondent said people should start saving for retirement at 29, two years older than the oldest of the generation. (If the survey findings in this bullet point and the previous one seem to contradict each other, you're reading them right.)
- Nearly half of Baby Boomers started saving at 35 or older.
- Half of Baby Boomers recommend people should start saving at 25 or younger.

But see what happens if you can keep your hands off that money for a longer period. It grows to $110,357 in 20 years, $237,175 in 30 years, and $464,286 in 40 years. Sounds like a lot to spring from $250 per month. And if you can earn 10% annual returns—admittedly, not an easy task—after 40 years the investment will have blossomed to more than $1.3 million. If you needed an incentive to start setting money aside today, now you've got it.

Of course, some younger readers might be thinking, "I'm a long way from retirement. Why not just spend the money now and start investing when I'm a little older?"

That's a reasonable question, and it's also one that's not very difficult to answer.

Consider identical twin brothers Jack and Joe. Their parents give them both the same financial advice—save enough to retire when you're 60. The brothers enter the work force at 18 with big dreams, but they choose different ways to pursue those goals.

Jack starts out saving immediately, living well below his means and investing $250 per month. He does this for the first 12 years of his work career, then stops because he wants to upgrade his lifestyle. Joe, on the other hand, figures he should have fun while he's young. Then, at age 30, just after Jack decides to stop saving, Joe gets started. Take a look at the following chart to see what happened.

Over the course of his working career, Jack invested $36,000 and Joe invested $93,000. Yet Jack ended up with nearly $250,000 more than Joe, assuming they invested their money at 8% a year. Once again, time flexes its muscles. The charts illustrating what happens when you set aside money early actually understate the potential benefits of starting early, because they don't take into account your ability to step up savings over time.

Age	JACK Annual Investment	JACK Value of Nest Egg, Invested at 8%	JOE Annual Investment	JOE Value of Nest Egg, Invested at 8%
18	$3,000	$3,000	$0	$0
19	$3,000	$6,240	$0	$0
20	$3,000	$9,739	$0	$0
21	$3,000	$13,518	$0	$0
22	$3,000	$17,600	$0	$0
23	$3,000	$22,008	$0	$0
24	$3,000	$26,768	$0	$0
25	$3,000	$31,910	$0	$0
26	$3,000	$37,463	$0	$0
27	$3,000	$43,460	$0	$0
28	$3,000	$49,936	$0	$0
29	$3,000	$56,931	$0	$0
30	$0	$61,486	$3,000	$3,000
31	$0	$66,405	$3,000	$6,240
32	$0	$71,717	$3,000	$9,739
33	$0	$77,455	$3,000	$13,518
34	$0	$83,651	$3,000	$17,600
35	$0	$90,343	$3,000	$22,008
36	$0	$97,570	$3,000	$26,768
37	$0	$105,376	$3,000	$31,910
38	$0	$113,806	$3,000	$37,463
39	$0	$122,911	$3,000	$43,460
40	$0	$132,743	$3,000	$49,936
41	$0	$143,363	$3,000	$56,931
42	$0	$154,832	$3,000	$64,486
43	$0	$167,218	$3,000	$72,645
44	$0	$180,596	$3,000	$81,456

	JACK		JOE	
Age	Annual Investment	Value of Nest Egg, Invested at 8%	Annual Investment	Value of Nest Egg, Invested at 8%
45	$0	$195,044	$3,000	$90,973
46	$0	$210,647	$3,000	$101,251
47	$0	$227,499	$3,000	$112,351
48	$0	$245,699	$3,000	$124,339
49	$0	$265,355	$3,000	$137,286
50	$0	$286,583	$3,000	$151,269
51	$0	$309,510	$3,000	$166,370
52	$0	$334,271	$3,000	$182,680
53	$0	$361,012	$3,000	$200,294
54	$0	$389,893	$3,000	$219,318
55	$0	$421,085	$3,000	$239,863
56	$0	$454,771	$3,000	$262,052
57	$0	$491,153	$3,000	$286,016
58	$0	$530,445	$3,000	$311,898
59	$0	$572,881	$3,000	$339,850
60	$0	$618,711	$3,000	$370,038

The previous examples have focused on retirement, in part because just about everyone will have to retire at some point, making it the most obvious savings goal for individuals. But most people will, over the course of their life, pursue several financial goals. Now it's time to identify the ones that matter to you.

Starting on the next page, you'll find ten common financial goals. Not all of them will apply to you today, and some may never be relevant. Still, don't dismiss any of the goals outright; give each of them some thought before you move on to the next.

Write down all the goals you either have for now or expect for the future. For each of those goals, estimate a time when you'll need the money to meet it.

If you haven't already started a personal-finance file, do it now. File away your financial goals, along with a copy of your budget, the sheet listing your worst financial problems, and any other relevant documents.

TEN COMMON FINANCIAL GOALS

When it comes to setting financial goals, know that you're not alone, and that there are a number of financial goals that people share. Here are 10 of the big ones:

1. Saving for emergencies.

Once you establish your budget, setting aside a small emergency fund should be priority one. Emergencies do happen, and no matter how detailed or how thoughtfully designed your budget is, it won't take into account every contingency. Start with $1,000, and set this aside even before you start to pay off high-interest debt.

That first $1,000 should provide you with some peace of mind; everyone feels better knowing they've got enough money in the bank to cover an unexpected expense. Over time, of course, you'll want to save more. Consider the $1,000 an acute emergency fund, something to cover an emergency-room visit or a call to the roofer to fix a leak. The next step will help you cope with longer-lasting emergencies. Call it a chronic emergency fund.

The most obvious chronic emergency would be the loss of a job—certainly an emergency by any measure. While financial experts disagree on an adequate size for an emergency fund, common targets range from three months of expenses to 12 months. Start with three, and try to build up to at least six.

Keep in mind, when you calculate a target for your emergency fund, you only need to consider the bottom portion of your budget. Forget what you bring home, just focus on the expenses. You're not trying to replace your income; you're just trying to fund your life until the crisis ends. Multiply your monthly expenses by three, then boost that number by 15% or so just to be conservative, and you've set a target for a three-month emergency fund. Want a six-month fund? Just double the first number.

2. Paying off credit cards or other consumer debt.

If you already carry consumer debt, then paying it off represents an immediate and pressing financial goal. According to data compiled by credit rating agencies, the average U.S. adult owes $4,878 in credit card debt—and this doesn't include store credit cards and charge cards that require users to maintain a $0 balance. Cards that normally carry a balance average debt of $8,220 per card.

While the average interest rate on credit cards with balances was 13.1% in August 2013, many cards charge rates of 18% or higher. Revolving debt—debt with no set payoff date—tends to carry higher interest rates than installment debt—loans with a fixed number of payments to satisfy the obligation.

3. Paying off student loans.

This type of debt deserves treatment separate from the consumer debt discussed above. Most student debt carries substantially lower interest rates than credit card debt. Given those lower rates and the large amounts owed by many borrowers, student-loan repayment probably requires a longer time commitment than do other types of debt.

Americans owe about $1 trillion in college loans—combining federal and private debt accrued by both students and parents—and the College Board estimates that the cost of a college education has risen 130% over the last 20 years. Costs continue to rise faster than inflation, and the problem of college debt isn't going away soon. Federal loans account for about 85% of the nation's education debt, and these loans offer several repayment options. For more information on those options, visit www.studentaid.ed.gov.

The key to success with student loan debt—and pretty much every other type of debt too large to pay off in six months or less—is consistency. If you set up a payment plan and stick with it, you can avoid penalties and other extra charges. Nationwide, the default rate on student loans is nearly 15%.

4. Supporting elderly parents.

The level of obligation in this area varies widely, affected by factors including the parents' wealth, health, and expectations, as well as the children's relationship with the parents.

These financial strictures often take people by surprise because the parties involved don't discuss the matter ahead of time. If you are a parent with adult children, bring up the topic. If you expect to be able to cover your retirement expenses, work it into the conversation. And if you can't cover your own retirement and you believe your children might be willing to help, then level with them.

If you are an adult with aging parents, you'd be wise to bring up the topic now rather than wait for circumstances to force it on you later. You know your own family better than anyone else, and no single piece of advice will fully address this touchy subject for everyone. But as a matter of course, asking either parents or children to chip in is both bad form and a recipe for familial discontent. Better to make no accusations or demands. Simply start up a discussion about retirement planning and see where it leads. Once again, recall the *personal* in personal finance.

5. Buying a new couch, stereo, or paint job for the house.

This category includes purchasing new assets or services that make an existing asset more valuable or more livable. For these purchases, the simple and obvious answer is the right one. Use your budget to help you set aside cash until you have enough to pay for them. Then deploy the cash.

Do you really need that new stereo today, knowing that you'll have to borrow to buy it and pay it off over time? Sure, you can probably get it for 90 days with no interest. But what if you forget to make a payment, or a more pressing expense crops up and consumes the money you'd earmarked to pay for the stereo. Then the 91st day arrives, and the interest payments you delayed but didn't avoid will hit like a hammer.

Don't take the risk. You don't have enough for the purchase until you can pay cash for it.

6. Buying a new car.

Few purchases inspire as much angst as buying a car, especially with the average car costing more than $31,000, according to TrueCar.com. Both sides of the financing debate make sense.

Pro-saving argument: "Cars don't appreciate in value, and you should never borrow to pay for something that won't rise in value over time."

Pro-borrowing argument: "A decent car costs $30,000, and my current vehicle won't last for the three years I'll need to set aside enough money to pay cash."

HOW TO CHOOSE AND PURCHASE A CAR

For most people, saving enough to buy a new car is impractical. But at the same time, if you purchase a car for $30,000 and finance it for five years at 4%, you'll take on a payment of more than $550 per month—a hit most people's budgets can't absorb without some amount of pain. Over those five years, you'll pay more than $3,100 in interest. The numbers are frightening, and they only get worse if you start to consider cars more expensive than the average. Check out the interest hit you'll take on pricier models, assuming you pay manufacturer's suggested retail prices for the base model. (This chart assumes a five-year loan at 4%.)

HOW MUCH WILL YOU REALLY PAY FOR THAT CAR?

	Monthly Payment	Total Cost	Interest Cost
2013 FORD F-150 PICKUP ($24,070)	$443	$26,597	$2,527
2013 HONDA ODYSSEY MINIVAN ($28,675)	$528	$31,685	$3,010
2013 CADILLAC ATS SEDAN ($33,095)	$609	$36,569	$3,474
2013 VOLVO S80 SEDAN ($39,150)	$721	$43,261	$4,111
2013 TOYOTA SEQUOIA SUV ($42,455)	$782	$46,912	$4,457
2013 BMW M3 SEDAN ($60,100)	$1,107	$66,410	$6,310
2013 MERCEDES-BENZ S-CLASS HYBRID ($92,350)	$1,701	$102,046	$9,696

Sources: www.motortrend.com, www.bankrate.com.

It's tough to attack either argument. However you decide to solve your transportation problems, you'll likely be better off if you save a few thousand before you need to make that decision. You probably don't need a new car today, but if you think you'll be in the market in the next, say, three years, start saving now.

In recent years, the cost of cars has driven Americans to hold onto their vehicles longer and put off new car purchases. Researcher R.L. Polk says that in the summer of 2013, the average car or light truck on the road was 11.4 years old, a record high. In 2002, the nation's fleet of light vehicles averaged 9.8 years old, and the age has risen for 11 consecutive years.

If you need a car and can't quickly set aside enough to pay cash, you have two options. Either finagle your expenses to find room for a hefty payment, or purchase a cheaper, used vehicle.

Yes, new cars are fun and sexy, and they smell nice. But for most people, they just cost too much. Used cars tend to require more maintenance than new cars, but not nearly enough to offset the drag of a new-car payment. A $100-a-month allocation for car repairs is much better than a $600-a-month line item for a car payment. Plus, you can always buy new car smell in a can.

7. Buying a house.

You'll read more on this topic in Chapter 8, but you might as well start thinking about it now. A house represents the largest purchase most Americans will ever make. Its blend of functionality and investment value separates it from any other type of purchase.

While some experts claim to know the proper age to purchase your first home, no single time is right for everyone. If you do wish to purchase a home someday, set a goal of saving a 20% down payment. The age of mortgages with no down payment has largely passed; it drowned in a sea of bad debt during the financial crisis that started in 2008 and has yet to fully shake itself out. Even if you can convince a bank to lend you money for a smaller down payment, a large one will reduce your housing costs in ways beyond simply reducing the amount borrowed.

8. Starting a business.

Some businesses require more start-up capital than others, and some people make better business owners than others. Do your own research into the business's needs—both financially and in terms of your own time and sweat—before you take the leap.

9. Buying a vacation home.

Admittedly, this goal will remain out of reach for most people. Even those who can afford a second home may be wiser not to make the purchase. But this goal lumps in with buying the private plane or the bass boat or assembling a collection of vintage cars.

While vacation properties and collections can appreciate in value, as investments they tend to underperform financial securities like stocks. Making money in collectibles requires both specialized knowledge and an element of luck. In addition, demand for luxury assets can dry up suddenly and remain low for long periods when times get tough; even rich people tend to cut back on spending during recessions, and delaying the purchase of a beachfront cottage or a touring boat is an easy choice.

Don't classify your vacation home or other expensive discretionary purchase as an investment to help justify the purchase. Sure, you might make your money back when you sell it, but you also might not. Before buying something extravagant, ensure that you have enough money to make the purchase without compromising your ability to reach other, likely more important, financial goals.

10. Retiring comfortably.

You've already seen some charts that address retirement savings, and you'll read more about saving for retirement in Chapter 7. For now, just remember that retirement remains your most important financial goal. If you meet all the others but fail to set aside enough to retire, you've missed the whole point.

Assuming you live long enough, at some point you'll retire and have to fund your lifestyle without a regular income. If you accumulate enough assets to create an income for yourself, the transition will prove less painful. You can't borrow to fund your retirement, so what you have is what you have. With that in mind, try very hard to have enough.

How much is enough? The table on the next page shows how long you can support your lifestyle at $50,000, $75,000, or $100,000 per year. The numbers assume you've built up a nest egg of $800,000, you retire at the end of your 65th year, and the investment grows at a rate of 2% per year after inflation.

In this example, the retiree supporting a $100,000-a-year lifestyle can afford seven full years of retirement, while the one who can live on $50,000 a year can make it 18 years, coming up short for the first time at age 84. Small changes can make a big difference here, and reducing the target budget to $45,000 a year will make the retirement portfolio last four more years.

Unless you're within 10 years of retirement, you may not know when you plan to retire or how much you'll need. You can adjust the retirement age and your target lifestyle when you get closer to the point when you want to stop working full-time. Just realize that the earlier you start and the more aggressively you control costs and set money aside, the better your chances to fund a long, strong retirement.

ANNUAL LIVING EXPENSES

AGE	Investment portfolio size		
	$100,000	**$75,000**	**$50,000**
65	$800,000	$800,000	$800,000
66	$716,000	$741,000	$766,000
67	$630,320	$680,820	$731,320
68	$542,926	$619,436	$695,946
69	$453,785	$556,825	$659,865
70	$362,861	$492,962	$623,063
71	$270,118	$427,821	$585,524
72	$175,520	$361,377	$547,234
73	$79,031	$293,605	$508,179
74	DEPLETED	$224,477	$468,343
75		$153,966	$427,709
76		$82,046	$386,264
77		$8,687	$343,989
78		DEPLETED	$300,869
79			$256,886
80			$212,024
81			$172,625
82			$131,256
83			$87,819
84			$42,210
85			DEPLETED

CHAPTER 5

CHANGING YOUR FINANCIAL PLAN

"Rather go to bed with out dinner
than to rise in debt."
—Benjamin Franklin

BY NOW YOU SHOULD UNDERSTAND at least some of the benefits of setting aside money at an early age. Those of you with a little gray around the temples—or a lot of gray everywhere—might be wishing you had a time machine about now. Fortunately, readers who discovered this book in their later years can use the same strategies to sort out their financial situation, cut costs, manage their money, and build wealth as younger folks. Never be afraid to change direction or to alter your existing plan once you find a better path.

While it's never too late to get started, no one of any age should consider tackling a task unless she is prepared to finish it. Remember, the job of money manager never really ends. While you should review your budget and your financial goals at least once a year for the rest of your life, some milestones deserve greater attention, in part because your budget and goals will probably change when they occur.

MILESTONES

JUNIOR YEAR OF HIGH SCHOOL

By this time, teenagers should know whether or not they intend to go to college, and if so, how much that college will cost. Teens and parents should discuss this issue honestly and in detail. Neither party will benefit unless both acknowledge how much they are prepared to invest in the child's college education.

Borrowing to pay for college makes sense in many cases, but too many stories about students with $150,000 in debt have come to light for a good money manager to simply assume that a college degree will always pay for itself. Both the parents and the student will make better decisions together than either will alone. College funding is addressed in more depth in Chapter 8, but for now, here are three important steps to take during a junior year of high school:

- Establish a checking account as the first step toward financial independence.
- Research college costs and potential salaries for different careers.
- Start investing if you have any income.

For those of you wondering why you're reading about milestones for a teenager, anyone old enough to earn income and spend it can benefit from preparing a budget.

FIRST YEAR OF COLLEGE

Regardless of whether the student pays for college or his parents do, everything changes this year. Income and expenses alter as the student adjusts to campus life, and a long-term picture starts to develop.

Teens' horizons tend to expand as they meet a larger swath of society during college. Thoughts of majors and internships inspire students to think more and more about their careers, which should in turn give them at least a rough idea of their earnings potential. At this point, any financial plan will likely lack both precision and permanence, but this part of a kid's life will teach him a lot about how the world works, and about the financial possibilities of that world. Important steps to take include:

- Fine-tune your budget in preparation for a few years of limited income potential.
- Seek internships to not only gain experience in a field that interests you, but also to learn how the professional world works.

JUNIOR YEAR IN COLLEGE

By now, the college student should be well into her major and have some ideas about career paths. This is another time when student and parents can benefit from each other's insights. At this point, the teen in particular will know enough about her strengths, weaknesses, and interests to flesh out her long-term financial goals. Juniors in college should:

- Continue to pursue internships.
- Draw on what you now know about your chosen field to expand on your financial goals.

FIRST YEAR AFTER COLLEGE

Remember how the early years of college taught kids about financial possibilities? Well, the first year of any new career offers a crash course in financial realities. The meeting of possibilities and realities can get messy, and it can sometimes be discouraging. For most young adults, the year after college graduation marks the first time they've needed to truly balance income and expenses with something more serious than an argument with parents at stake. During the first year after college:

- Completely revamp your budget. Talk to your parents or another trusted adult to gain insight on tackling expenses and meeting obligations you may never have faced before.
- Don't make knee-jerk changes to your financial plan just because you're having trouble making ends meet. You won't meet your long-term goals overnight, and that's why they're called long-term goals.
- Consider disability insurance to replace your income if you become sick or injured.
- Contribute to your employer's retirement plan. If your employer doesn't provide a plan, fund your own individual retirement arrangement (IRA).
- Get renter's insurance. Even if you don't own anything but a moth-eaten blanket and a single coffee mug, you need the policy to protect you against liability claims if anything bad happens in your apartment. Is it likely? No. But the whole point of insurance is to protect you against things that are unlikely to happen yet too expensive to deal with if they do. Independent Insurance Agents & Brokers of America estimates the average cost of renter's insurance at $12 per month for a policy including $30,000 in property coverage and $100,000 in liability coverage.

CAREER CHANGE

Depending on how you define a career change, most of us will make them several times in our lives. Not every career change is as drastic as a truck driver quitting to become an accountant. But if you gain a promotion to management, or start your own business, or make a lateral move to a new job within a company, your long-term earnings potential may change. Any time you switch jobs, and especially if the new position carries a different salary or new responsibilities, you must revisit both your budget and your sheet of financial goals. Repeat this process every time you make a career change.

- Make a realistic assessment of your future income potential.
- Review your insurance coverage to ensure that your disability and health insurance remain in force.
- If you change employers, transfer your retirement account from the previous employer to either your new employer's plan or your personal IRA.

ENGAGEMENT

Before you get married—preferably before you propose—talk money with your prospective spouse. You don't have to agree on everything. But if one spouse socks away 40% of their income and eats just two meals a day to save money, while the other spends most of their disposable income on entertainment, the marriage will start out at a huge disadvantage.

A study by a Kansas State University researcher found that couples who argued about money during the early stages of their relationship were more likely to divorce later on. Another study by a Utah State University researcher found that couples who disagreed about finances more than once a week were 30% more likely to divorce than couples who disagreed just a few times a month. The second study also found that consumer debt after the wedding contributed to the instability of the marriage.

The lovebirds mentioned above—the ones with the drastically different ideas about spending—seem likely to argue about money. Address such differences of opinion as early as possible and find some middle ground. Your marriage will benefit from it.

- Revamp the budget to include any new income or expense items.
- Coordinate health and auto insurance coverage.
- Consider purchasing life insurance.

PREGNANCY

Children cost money. Now, that's not meant to be an indictment of parenthood or a reason not to have kids, because the rewards of parenthood are not measured in dollars. However, do take the costs into account. A U.S. Department of Agriculture report from August 2013 estimated that a middle-income couple will spend more than $240,000 to raise a child for 18 years.

The numbers get big in a hurry, but you still should not panic. Somehow, couples have managed to raise children for generations without going broke. If you want—or need—to spend less than the national average, you probably can. And every parent learns on the job, so don't worry if you go through a couple iterations before you come up with a solid plan.

Of course, any plan should include setting aside a small but regular amount for kid-specific expenditures, as well as an allowance for larger expenses in the future like summer camps, a trombone for the high school band, and eventually college.

- Update your budget to reflect new line items.
- Revisit your insurance coverage to ensure the child's needs are met.
- Write a will and establish a guardian for the child in the event something happens to you.
- Start contributing to a college fund.

CHILDREN MOVING OUT

At this stage, your financial needs may decline, particularly if you've paid off a house. Focus on retiring student-loan debt, if you have any, and saving for retirement.

- Modify the budget again, this time to reflect the lack of child-specific expenses and cuts to allocations for costs like food, which should now decline with fewer mouths to satisfy.
- Firm up the financial plan for your retirement years. Once you've established specific goals, pursue them with vigor.

TEN YEARS BEFORE RETIREMENT

At this point, you should have a good idea about whether the financial goals you set years ago and have modified several times since will actually do the trick. By assessing the state of your portfolio, you should know whether or not you're likely to reach those goals.

At this point you should possess a fairly clear picture of the amount of money you'll need to fund your retirement. Remember the example of how long money will last based on whether you withdraw $50,000, $75,000, or $100,000 per year? Until now, your target withdrawal rate represented little more than an estimate. Now, however, you can convert that estimate into a practical plan.

- Make arrangements for postretirement health-care coverage.
- Look into long-term care or other arrangements for your later years.
- Revisit your will and any retirement assets that may end up in the hands of your beneficiaries.

No matter your stage in life, a good plan will help you reach the next stage with your finances intact. As you've learned, financial goals and strategies will change over time. Don't fear such developments. No plan—no matter how well-conceived—will work forever.

All that said, you can hang your hat on a few core principles that will never change, even when everything else does. Here are just three of them:

1. Nobody else cares as much about your financial health as you do.
2. Good money managers get as much satisfaction out of wanting less as they do out of having more.
3. Even under the best of circumstances, debt is dangerous.

While this book addressed the first two principles at some length in Part 1, so far it has barely touched on the third. And number three is a doozy.

DIGGING INTO DEBT

To borrow, or not to borrow, that is the question. Consumers never stop tiring of asking that question, even though they already know the answer. Scottrade's 2012 American Retirement Survey asked consumers about borrowing, and their responses should surprise no one.

- 40% of respondents said nonmortgage debt caused them to save less for retirement than they did the previous year, well up from the 33% who gave the same answer in the 2011 survey.
- With debt cited as a chief reason, 93% said they would take steps in 2012 to address their financial situation.
- 42% said they planned to pay down debts in 2012 (up from 39% in 2011) and 38% said they would reduce their credit-card spending (up from 35% in 2011).

Consumers seem to understand the dangers of excessive borrowing, and they intend to do something about it. Yet somehow consumer debt never seems to trend lower for long. According to the Federal Reserve, total consumer credit—excluding mortgages and a few other types of loans—dipped slightly in 2009, probably sparked by the recession. However, between 2009 and 2012, total consumer debt rose nearly 15%.

Total consumer credit fell slightly in the first half of 2013, but don't expect the trend to continue. Credit use has trended generally higher for decades. Remember those stats from the Federal Reserve cited in Chapter 1? U.S. consumers have racked up debt equivalent to about $9,300 for every man, woman, and child. And as of mid-2013, consumer debt accounted for more than 11% of household assets, versus just 8.5% 25 years ago.

Debt, once considered a foolish indulgence at best and a moral scourge at worst, has over the years transformed into a consumer product many people can no longer live without. While consumers worldwide acknowledge the risks of borrowing, a "Do as I say, not as I do" attitude has taken hold. Against that backdrop, you and your budget may seem to stand alone.

But you are not alone.

High-profile financial advisers like Suze Orman, Dave Ramsey, and others have shouted to the hills about the dangers of debt, making many of the same arguments used by today's critics, as well as those hundreds—and in some cases thousands—of years ago. In the following pages you'll hear from some of those debt-decrying pundits, but next on the agenda is actually answering the question: To borrow, or not to borrow?

The answer depends almost entirely on one thing: whether or not the product or service will increase in value or allow you to make more money.

GOOD DEBT VERSUS BAD DEBT

Plenty of people maintain that there is no such thing as good debt. Given the massive $12 trillion debt load for U.S. households and nonprofit organizations, it takes a nuanced argument to rebut the "no debt under any circumstances" crowd. That said, here are four types of debt that, if managed correctly, qualify as good debt:

1. Mortgages

The real-estate crash of the last decade still lingers in the minds of American consumers, and the housing market continues to struggle. The housing bubble began to burst in 2006, ending a 25-year upward march. Prices have risen since the start of 2012, but the Federal Housing Finance Agency's U.S. Home Price Index remains well below prerecession peaks.

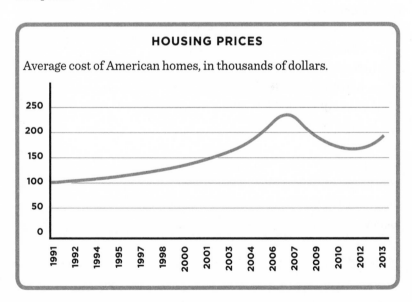

HOUSING PRICES

Average cost of American homes, in thousands of dollars.

However, the last few years stand out as an anomaly, a painful reversal of a longstanding positive trend. Over the next decade, home prices should rise gradually, as they typically have.

Since homes appreciate in value, and since they cost far more than the average person can afford to purchase with cash, mortgage loans qualify as good debt. Mostly.

Caveats:

- Mortgage loan terms vary greatly. You'll learn more about this in Chapter 8, but in general you want to keep the interest rate low and try to borrow for a term of no more than 15 or 20 years, rather than the standard 30 years.
- Budget very carefully before committing to a home purchase. Housing represents the largest line item on most individuals' budgets, and if you buy more than you can afford, the home's rise in price won't staunch your hemorrhaging cash flow.
- Never listen to anyone else's assessment of what you can afford. When a bank or mortgage company says you can afford a $250,000 home, what they mean is that based on your credit profile, they believe you can take on that loan without defaulting. However, the lenders in no way have your financial interests at heart. Let your budget and your financial plan tell you whether or not you can afford the house.

2. Business loans

In some cases, borrowing to start or expand a business makes sense. But way too many businesses go bust for business loans to qualify as good debt without some caveats.

Before you even think about borrowing to start or expand a business, cover all your bases. Prepare a business plan that includes realistic cash-flow projections, conservative projections for expenses, and personal information about your business experience and financial condition that will make a banker want to partner with you. You can improve your odds if you approach a bank that already knows you. Still, your business plan and your credit history will do the heavy lifting.

The Small Business Administration (www.sba.gov) provides a wealth of information about business loans. Use their resources to prepare before you fill out any loan applications. The SBA offers loan-guarantee programs, but it won't backstop just any loan. The agency will want to see much of the same information your banker expects.

Caveats:

- Unlike the case with a home loan, you should at least partially rely on the advice of the banker offering you a business loan. Home loans are backed by the value of the asset—in the case of mortgages, the house—and the bank can foreclose on the asset and resell it to recoup its losses. Business loans rarely work that way, so banks have a vested interest in ensuring your business can cover the payments.
- Be honest with yourself about the business. Consider the economic conditions, the success rate of similar businesses, and your own suitability to run a business. The skills required to run a remodeling company differ greatly from the skills of a world-class carpenter. Many would-be entrepreneurs assume that their expertise in their specialty will translate into an ability to finance a business and market their services. Such assumptions can be dangerous.
- Expect the bank to draw heavily on your personal assets as collateral for the loan. If you have nothing but expertise, few banks will accept the risk of lending you money to start a business that could fail.

3. College

By just about any measure, college graduates have it better than those without postsecondary education. The unemployment rate for college grads consistently remains below that for other workers. In addition, in 2011 college grads averaged salaries 85% higher than people who didn't attend. However, not all college degrees are created equal, particularly if you must borrow to obtain them.

By now you've probably spotted the theme. Even good debt isn't good unless the conditions are right. In the case of college degrees, students and parents should consider the earning power the degree will provide, as well as the financial condition of whoever takes out the loan. You'll learn more about providing for college in Chapter 8.

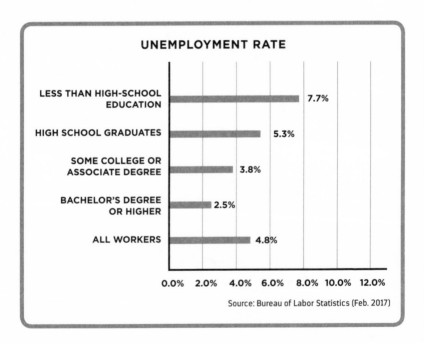

UNEMPLOYMENT RATE

LESS THAN HIGH-SCHOOL EDUCATION — 7.7%
HIGH SCHOOL GRADUATES — 5.3%
SOME COLLEGE OR ASSOCIATE DEGREE — 3.8%
BACHELOR'S DEGREE OR HIGHER — 2.5%
ALL WORKERS — 4.8%

0.0% 2.0% 4.0% 6.0% 8.0% 10.0% 12.0%

Source: Bureau of Labor Statistics (Feb. 2017)

Caveats:

- Unless you plan to enter a high-wage field like business or engineering, you will probably end up in trouble if you graduate owing more than your first year's salary. Borrowing $100,000 to earn a degree that will get you a $40,000-a-year job is a recipe for years of belt-tightening.

- Remember that student loan debt never goes away. You can't get rid of it by declaring bankruptcy. And with more than $1 trillion in loans outstanding, expect lenders to collect aggressively.

- Don't make a decision about college loans until you've exhausted other forms of funding. Federal and state aid and scholarships can provide thousands of dollars of assistance for college students. The needy receive priority for most federal grants, but plenty of families who would consider themselves in the middle class can tap into federal or state funds.

4. Home-equity loans

These loans allow individuals to borrow against the equity in their homes. In other words, if you owe $150,000 on a home with a market value of $200,000, you've built up $50,000 in equity. Lenders know that if the buyer defaults, the home can be sold to repay the money.

At first blush, home equity loans look like good debt. After all, they borrow on an asset that increases in value over time. But they also represent a risk in the sense that you give a creditor a claim on that asset.

If you take out a home-equity loan to fund repairs or remodeling projects that will preserve or increase the home's value, then the loan may make sense—assuming your budget can absorb the payment. The trouble comes when homeowners tap into their equity to get rid of credit card debt and other consumer obligations. In theory, this makes sense—trading bad debt for so-called good debt—and home-equity loans tend to charge lower interest rates than credit cards.

Using a home-equity loan to retire other debt only makes sense for consumers with the discipline to avoid digging the same hole. Unless you are 100% prepared to cut up your credit cards and swear off borrowing any money for any reason, don't allow your consumer-borrowing mistakes to cost you your home.

Caveats:

- Rates and terms on home-equity loans vary widely from lender to lender. Shop around and pay attention to the fine print.
- In general, you should avoid loans that charge variable interest rates, which rise and fall based on changes in a benchmark rate. In late 2013, interest rates languished near historical lows, and the risk of rates rising in the years ahead was very high. Even in an environment with higher interest rates, you take a risk when you bet on their future direction.
- There's a reason mortgage lenders want homeowners to provide a generous down payment. The closer the loan value is to the total value of the house, the riskier the loan, and thus the higher the interest rate. Home-equity lenders often play close to the danger line, so be careful not to overextend yourself.

WHEN GOOD DOESN'T REALLY MEAN GOOD

You must have noticed all the caveats connected to the different types of *good* debt you can acquire. All debt carries risk, even the loans you take out for legitimate reasons. Unless you keep firm control of your debt, it can—no, it will—turn on you.

Be warned. Even some of the best money managers have lost control at times. Take real estate investor and U.S. President Donald Trump. Even a man with his wealth can't always stay on top. Companies bearing the Trump name have declared bankruptcy multiple times. Each time, Trump turned to the bankruptcy court because he couldn't pay his debts, and each time he rose to wealth again.

It's a nice plan if you can pull it off, but most individuals don't get more than two chances. If you're like many people, you've already blown one. According to the Administrative Office of the U.S. Courts, there were 1.4 million nonbusiness bankruptcy filings in 2009, or roughly one for every 100 households.

So keep a lid on the debt, because borrowing can be hazardous to your wealth. Speaking of hazards, turn to Chapter 6, where you can explore the murky world of *bad* debt.

BORROWING TROUBLE

"The modern theory of the perpetuation of debt
has drenched the earth with blood, and crushed its
inhabitants under burdens ever accumulating."

—Thomas Jefferson

BAD DEBT HAS ONLY ONE ADVANTAGE over the good debt discussed in Chapter 5: the danger is easier to spot. In fact, with most types of bad debt, the risks leap out at you. As such, these debts require no caveats. Still, only you can bridge the gap between seeing the danger and avoiding it. Hold your hand tightly over your wallet as you check out six kinds of bad debt.

Store credit. No matter what the store sells, you have no business taking out a loan (and yes, a line of credit is, for practical purposes, a loan) from a retail establishment. If you can't afford to buy it without making installment payments, then you can't afford it. Many store credit lines/credit cards charge obscenely high interest rates. Just save up for the item and pay cash.

Credit cards. With very few exceptions, credit cards cause more trouble than they're worth. Remember that in late 2013 the average card charged 13% interest, and many charged much more. In contrast, you could obtain a 30-year home mortgage for less than 4.5%. Consumer debt of all types tends to cost more than debt backed by real estate. And because you pay credit cards on a revolving basis rather than through installments, retiring the debt requires more initiative.

Credit cards charge minimum payments designed to cover the interest cost and a small amount of the principal, or the balance owed. Because the card companies make money only when you maintain a balance on the card, they have no incentive to help you repay the loan. In some cases, cards set the minimum payment such that if you only pay that much and never use the card again, it could take years to pay off the debt.

For instance: Say you owe $10,000 on a credit card that charges 18% annual interest (1.5% a month) and requires a minimum payment of 3% of the balance. If you pay the minimum every month, you'll take more than 20 years to pay it off, along the way racking up more than $9,600 in interest charges. As your balance declines, so will the minimum payment. If instead you start with a $300 payment—the 3% minimum for a $10,000 balance—and keep sending that amount even as the balance declines, you'll pay the card off in less than four years.

PAYING OFF A CREDIT CARD

Assuming a credit card balance of $10,000 and an 18% interest rate, here's how long it will take to pay the card off.

Payment	Months to Pay Off	Total Payoff	Interest Cost
3% MINIMUM	244	$19,698	$9,698
$300 PER MONTH	46	$13,665	$3,665
$500 PER MONTH	23	$11,471	$1,471

Source: Bankrate.com

Stacked up against such scary numbers, the amenities of some credit cards—frequent-flier miles, retail credits, and cash back—just don't mean much. Don't fall prey to a card that pays you back. Lenders are in business to collect money from consumers, not pay them, and the companies wouldn't offer the promotion unless it improved their bottom line. Think about the business model. A company collects 18% from you, then gives you 1% back, and you think you're getting a deal? Think again.

Remember how you shouldn't let a mortgage lender tell you how much house you can afford? That warning goes double for credit card companies—don't let them determine your payment. Instead, pay more than the minimum, and keep paying it until the debt melts away.

Borrowing to buy consumable goods. Yes, this overlaps the first two bad-debt items, but it warrants some extra discussion. By now you already know that using credit to purchase assets that decline in value makes little sense. However, it takes a special kind of foolish to borrow money to purchase consumables, or products like clothing that may lose more than half of their value overnight. If you charge lunch on a credit card, then fail to pay that card off, you could literally be paying for that burger every month for years. No meal tastes that good.

Car loans. As you learned in Chapter 4, new cars are simply too expensive for most people to finance, and that's assuming you use a reputable lender and nab a nice interest rate. Plenty of dealerships offer their own financing, and it can leave you worse off than if you'd gone to a bank.

Now, you may be thinking, "But what if I get a good deal on a car? Can't my negotiating skills make up for the cost of the loan?"

To put it simply, no.

At most car lots, the finance office is a major revenue center. Dealerships wouldn't finance cars if the contracts didn't make money for them. For those of you who "beat the system" by leasing rather than buying outright, did you know that dealers on average make more money on lease contracts than they do on straight financing? Since only the buyer and seller enter into the lease contract, somebody has to provide that extra profit, and it sure isn't the seller.

Sometimes dealers offer you what sounds like attractive financing after persuading you to overpay for the car, and sometimes they mark down the car and make it back on the financing. Sometimes they win on both ends. Don't forget that car dealers sell and finance cars for a living. Would you walk into an operating room and assume you could do a better job on your own gallbladder surgery than the guy in the scrubs with the scalpel? Of course not. Anyone who walks into a car dealership expecting to beat the experts at their own game is fooling themselves. Sure, you might get a better deal than your neighbor, but that still doesn't necessarily make it a *good* deal.

Payday loans or advances on tax refunds. The interest rates on these loans can be astronomical. While most payday loans average annual percentage rates (APRs)—the actual yearly cost of a loan over its life—of about 400%, some charge as much as 5,000%. That said, never commit to a loan of any kind based on an interest rate that doesn't include an APR. For instance, a payday loan office may advance you $300 for $30, which means you owe $330 in two weeks. That $30 fee equates to 10% per two weeks, or an APR of 260%. Plenty of people might pay the $30, but most would balk at the 260% APR, which is why short-term loan companies de-emphasize the APR.

Payday loans deliver convenience for a price (and it's a really high price). You're much better off to start saving early and go with an emergency fund instead. It's a lot cheaper.

Any loan from (or to) a friend or family member. Money changes relationships. Ambrose Bierce defined debt as "An ingenious substitute for the chain and whip of the slave driver." Sure, plenty of people borrow from friends or family, pay it back, and go on without anything bad happening. But plenty others place themselves in a position of subservience that can make both the borrower and the lender uncomfortable.

DEALING WITH DEBT

Now you know how to tell good debt from bad debt. Bad debt is like a cobra that sees you standing between itself and a yummy rat, while good debt is like a cobra that probably won't bite you if you hand the rat over immediately and promise to deliver another one tomorrow. Regardless, you should always be careful with debt—particularly consumer debt—and you should do without it as much as possible. However, with about two-thirds of U.S. families in possession of a credit card, most people have already taken on some debt.

The 2013 Consumer Financial Literacy Survey found 37% of Americans carry credit card debt from month to month, down from 39% last year and 44% in 2009. While the decline in borrowers running balances is encouraging, the numbers still suggest that more than half of consumers who carry credit cards regularly pay interest on purchases they've made in the past.

Interest payments aren't like allocations for food or the light bill. When you pay the electric company or you head to the grocery store, you receive a tangible benefit. You pay your bill and the lights stay on, or you plunk down a few bucks and come home with eggs and a gallon of milk. Interest is an invisible bill that keeps you paying for the echo of a past benefit.

While experts disagree on what constitutes a *reasonable* amount of debt, one common rule of thumb is 28/36. In other words, housing expenses shouldn't account for more than 28% of your gross income, while housing and other debts combined shouldn't account for more than 36%. Still, a 36% debt burden for someone earning $50,000 per year equates to $1,500 per month—meaning up to $333 in consumer debt payments. Could someone earning $50,000 per year handle such payments? Probably, particularly if the person budgets well. But just because you can handle the debt payments doesn't mean you should borrow.

Besides, only you can determine what's reasonable for you. And many already strain under an unreasonable debt burden. If you fall into that group, you are not alone, and you should not be without hope. The fact that you've read this far, that you've created a budget, and that you've committed to living by its precepts, suggests that you have what it takes to get out of debt.

Now that we've looked at the different types of good and bad debts, as well as their dangers, you're ready for a five-step program that can get anyone out of debt.

FIVE STEPS TO FREEDOM FROM DEBT

Before you check out step one, understand that getting out of debt is like a lot of multistep programs; you won't make it all the way down the path to dumping debt if you skip a step, or if you turn back. You will get out of debt by deciding to change your behavior. Once you make that commitment, the steps simply point the way.

STEP 1: STOP BORROWING MONEY

No new credit card purchases. No store credit. No new loans of any kind. Period.

If you aren't willing to take this step, you're probably not actually ready to get out of debt. Use your budget and live within your means. If you can't afford something, make do without it.

STEP 2: COVER ALL YOUR NECESSARY EXPENSES FIRST

Never put a dime toward the principal of a loan until you've covered the expenses you truly need to live: housing, food, clothing, and transportation to and from work. When you get down to it, everything else is discretionary (though for most of us, living without phone service might be difficult, and canceling insurance policies might be foolish). You know which line items on your budget reflect needs and which are wants. Scour the budget and create a baseline level of expenditures you cannot compromise. These expenditures include your installment payments and the minimum payments for any revolving debt.

Everything else is fair game. Dip into entertainment and other discretionary categories if you can and come up with a monthly amount you can use to pay down your debt above and beyond the minimum payments.

STEP 3: DON'T TAP YOUR EMERGENCY FUND

Yes, it can be tempting. If you've set aside that $1,000 emergency fund, it would sure look nice in a check to one of your creditors. Still, resist the urge.

The emergency fund exists to deal with emergencies, addressing unexpected costs without disrupting your budget. If you deploy your emergency fund to pay off debt, what happens if an emergency comes up? More than likely, you'd end up creating more debt to cover it. Financially, that would put you back where you started, but it would feel a lot more like you took a step backward. Let the emergency fund do its job, so you can focus on destroying your debt.

STEP 4: START YOUR DEBT SNOWBALL MOVING

Now it's time to start the ball rolling. Prepare a spreadsheet (or hard copy) with all of your debts outside of your mortgage. Write down the total amount owed, the interest rate charged, and the minimum payment.

Some financial advisers recommend starting with the debt with the highest interest rate. But when it comes to paying off debt, momentum matters, and the taste of success will drive you to pursue your goal even more aggressively. So start with the one you can pay off most quickly. This process is called a snowball because, just as a snowball grows as it rolls downhill, so will your ability to pay off debt. To start a debt snowball, you need two things.

First, you need a surplus. Second, you need to ensure the amount you currently apply toward debt payoff will continue to serve that purpose until you've eradicated every credit account. As you pay off one account, the money used to pay that account jumps to the second account, creating an ever-enlarging snowball.

By way of example, consider Millie, Jimmy's little sister. She was so impressed by Jimmy's financial housecleaning that she created her own budget. But unlike Jimmy, Millie pays on a number of credit accounts. The table on the next page shows Millie's credit accounts, collected in a debt-snowball worksheet. After cutting her budget, Millie cleared up $250 per month to beef up her debt payoff.

MILLIE'S DEBT SNOWBALL: PHASE 1

	Balance	APR	Minimum Payment
STORE ACCOUNT	$60	12%	$10
CREDIT CARD 1	$450	19%	$25
CREDIT CARD 2	$700	13%	$50
AUTO LOAN	$3,350	6.5%	$300
STUDENT LOAN	$14,000	5%	$250
TOTAL MINIMUM PAYMENTS			$635
MONTHLY SURPLUS			$250
TOTAL DEBT PAYOFF			$885

After lining up the accounts in order from the smallest balance to the largest, Millie is horrified to learn the minimum payments she's making eat up $635 each month. No wonder she lies awake at night worrying about her finances. As tempting as it would be to pay off a few of the smaller accounts and use the freed-up money to loosen the straits somewhere else in the budget, Millie won't do it. Going forward she's committed to pouring that $635—plus her newly found $250 surplus—into an all-out debt offensive.

The next table shows what happens after the first month. As soon as she created the debt snowball worksheet, she sent out checks. Millie applied $50 from her surplus to the department store account. Combined with the $10 she'd already allocated for the minimum payment, she paid the account off. The remaining $200 from the surplus went onto the first credit card.

When the next statements arrived, Millie recorded the Month 2 balances, which subtracted her payments, then added the month's interest charges.

MILLIE'S DEBT SNOWBALL: PHASE 2

	Balance	APR	Minimum Payment	Month 1 Payment	Month 2 Balance
STORE ACCOUNT	$60	12%	$10	$60	$0
CREDIT CARD 1	$450	19%	$25	$225	$232
CREDIT CARD 2	$700	13%	$50	$50	$658
AUTO LOAN	$3,350	6.5%	$300	$300	$3,068
STUDENT LOAN	$14,000	5%	$250	$250	$13,808
TOTAL MINIMUM PAYMENTS			$635	$625	
MONTHLY SURPLUS			$250	$260	
TOTAL DEBT PAYOFF			$885	$885	

Admittedly, it looks like interest charges never stop accruing. But they do stop—when the debt is paid off. And there truly is no feeling quite like sending a credit account to that zero balance in the sky.

Which brings us to:

STEP 5: REVEL IN YOUR SUCCESS, THEN REPEAT IT

The first time you pay off a credit account, pat yourself on the back, do a happy dance, or call your friends and tell them all about it. Celebrate, because you've accomplished something. Just don't fall into the trap of rewarding yourself with something expensive. Sure, that strategy makes sense for some accomplishments, but not this one. You're not yet finished, but you've taken a strong first step.

After you finish your happy dance, follow Millie's example and try to hit the same target a second time. Flush with excitement over paying off the department store account, she cancels it immediately and starts planning for the next month. With the $10 minimum payment on the store account no longer needed, she adds that $10 to the monthly surplus.

The next table shows what happened in Months 2, 3, 4, and 5. In Month 2, Millie paid off the first credit card, courtesy of the $25 minimum payment augmented by $207 from the surplus. The remaining $53 surplus went toward the second credit card.

By paying off the first credit card, Millie moved its $25 minimum payment into the surplus for Month 3, boosting it to $285 per month. By Month 4, Millie had paid off the second credit card, with enough left over to throw an extra $102 onto the auto loan.

At the rate Millie is going, she'll pay off the auto loan in Month 8. Then she can attack the student loan at a rate of $885 per month, retiring it in just two years.

Now those are some impressive numbers. By committing an extra $250 per month to her debts, she paid off nearly $19,000 in less than two years. Suppose she had instead just paid the minimum payments? And

MILLIE'S DEBT SNOWBALL: PHASE 3

	Balance	APR	Minimum Payment	Month 1 Payment	Month 2 Balance
STORE ACCOUNT	$60	12%	$10	$60	$0
CREDIT CARD 1	$450	19%	$25	$225	$232
CREDIT CARD 2	$700	13%	$50	$50	$658
AUTO LOAN	$3,350	6.5%	$300	$300	$3,068
STUDENT LOAN	$14,000	5%	$250	$250	$13,808
TOTAL MINIMUM PAYMENTS			$635	$625	
MONTHLY SURPLUS			$250	$260	
TOTAL DEBT PAYOFF			$885	$885	

suppose that when she paid off a debt, she just allocated the money into entertainment or dining out, rather than snowballing the other credit accounts? At that rate, the student loan wouldn't have been paid off until the sixth year.

You can't understand how it feels to be debt-free until you get there. Words just don't cut it. Think of finally putting down a heavy weight you've borne for far too long, or of a grip around your neck finally loosening, and you have an idea. The freedom is amazing.

THE MYSTERIOUS CREDIT SCORE

Paying off consumer debt will affect more than just your mental health. You should see an improvement in your credit score as well. Almost everyone has a credit score, but few seem to know why it's as high or as low as it is. Most people don't even know their credit rating. The 2013 Financial Literacy Survey revealed that in 2012, 65% of adults hadn't reviewed their credit report, and 60% hadn't checked their credit score.

Month 2 Payment	Month 3 Balance	Month 3 Payment	Month 4 Balance	Month 4 Payment	Month 5 Balance
$232	$0				
$103	$562	$335	$233	$233	$0
$300	$2,785	$300	$2,500	$402	$2,111
$250	$13,616	$250	$13,423	$250	$13,229
$625		$600		$600	
$260		$285		$285	
$885		$885		$885	

Your credit score has an impact on whether or not banks will lend you money and how much interest you'll pay if they do. These days, more and more businesses access credit scores because they connect low scores with risky behavior. Fair Isaac claims its FICO credit score is used in more than 90% of lending decisions. And if bankers are checking it out, so should you. Scores range from 300 to 850, with high scores better than low ones. Your credit score can also impact your insurance premium, as well as a company's decision of whether or not to offer you a job.

All of the factors that generate the credit score will be reflected in your credit report, revealing a financial history of your life. Three credit-reporting agencies—TransUnion, Equifax, and Experian—collect this information. Even if you haven't been paying attention to how you've used money, the credit-reporting agencies (commonly called credit bureaus) have.

ANATOMY OF A CREDIT SCORE

According to MyFICO.com, five factors contribute to your credit score:

Payment history (35% of the score). Lenders prefer borrowers who pay their bills on time.

Amounts owed (30%). FICO considers the number of accounts with bal-ances and the percentage of your total credit that you currently use, with particular attention paid to credit cards and other revolving accounts.

Length of credit history (15%). While a longer credit history makes for a higher credit score, it isn't a necessity if you score well in the other areas.

Types of credit (10%). FICO seems to favor people with multiple types of accounts, but at some point (FICO provides few details), a high number of accounts will start hurting your score.

New credit (10%). If you've opened multiple credit accounts in a short time, FICO will deem you a greater risk.

When you fall too far behind on a loan payment, many creditors will inform the credit-reporting agencies. These companies don't catch everything, but if you've defaulted on a loan, made too many late utility payments, or moved out of an apartment without paying the last month's rent, your credit reports probably show it—and every company that reviews those reports will probably know it.

Good money managers keep an eye on their credit reports, in part to assess how well they're doing and why their credit score has risen or fallen, and in part because sometimes credit-reporting agencies make mistakes. If an agency gets the facts wrong, visit its website and fill out an online form asking it to fix the problem.

Under certain circumstances, the credit-reporting agencies must provide you with free reports, and plenty of websites will offer to obtain reports for you. However, most will charge fees. Don't bother jumping through any hoops. Visit AnnualCreditReport.com, and you can obtain all three credit reports at no cost once a year. Try ordering one now, then a second in four months, and the third four months after that. Keep up that cycle, and you'll never lose track of your credit picture. You'll find the information enlightening, and you'll know what everyone else sees when they look at you. Depending on the state of your credit, this may not make you feel good, but at least you'll know where you stand.

PART 3

Looking Ahead

CHAPTER 7
INVESTING IN YOUR FUTURE

"If you aim at nothing, you will hit it every time."
—Zig Ziglar

IF YOU'VE MADE IT THIS FAR, then only one question remains: where do you want to end up? This question extends far beyond your finances, and permeates many elements of your future and your life.

By now you've constructed a budget that will help you cope with the pressures of here and now. In addition, you've learned skills that will allow your budget to grow with you and change along with your circumstances.

That's good.

You've also devised a financial plan that peers into the future. It reflects your goals and dreams, your hopes and fears. It takes courage to plan ahead, because nobody knows what will happen when you get older. Yet, despite the uncertainty, you've attempted to plan for retirement, as well as all the milestones you'll reach before you get there.

That's even better, but you're still missing a piece of this puzzle.

Think of your financial plan as a map with a series of X's marked at important junctures of life, and imagine your budget as the car that can transport you to and from those X's. All you need now is fuel—something to power your car along your journey. Without fuel, your car won't get far. And when the fuel is money, you would be wise to consider an investment portfolio that grows over time. Fortunately, you already know plenty about investing, because you already invest. Everyone does. (Yes, this statement even applies to those who have never even read a newspaper's business section.)

When you picked up this book, you invested your time in learning about finance. Every time you take a class at night, turn down overtime at work to attend your child's Scout meeting, or take your sweetheart out for dinner on date night even though your favorite show is on, you make an investment decision. You're sacrificing today's currency—time, money, and recreation—to cultivate future growth. It may sound strange, but if you know how to invest in a relationship, you have the ability to invest financially. All you need is a little perspective.

Unrealistic expectations can torpedo investors as easily as bad decisions. So before you invest, you need to understand what to expect from your investments. The Rule of 72 offers a quick-and-dirty tool. Here's how it works:

RULE OF 72

See how long it will take your investment to double in value.

Investment Growth Rate	Number of Years to Double in Value
4%	18
6%	12
8%	9
10%	7
12%	6

Divide your investment's expected annual return into 72, and find out roughly how long it will take to double your money. In other words, if you grow your money at 6% a year, it will double in about 12 years. Bump the growth up to 8% annually, and you can double the money in approximately nine years, helped by the power of compound interest.

The Rule of 72 applies only to money already invested. As the charts back in Chapter 4 showed, you can drastically increase the value of your investments by adding money to the portfolio on a regular basis.

At this point the question isn't whether to invest—you know you should—nor is the question how much you should invest—your budget will tell you how much you can spare. The biggest issue outstanding is *how* to invest. In the following paragraphs, you'll learn about the three best-known types of financial investments: stocks, bonds, and mutual funds.

WHAT TO INVEST IN

STOCKS

Common stocks represent ownership of a tiny piece of a company. The price of the stock rises and falls along with the company's business performance and prospects. In general, if a company grows its sales and profits consistently, it will rise in value over time. However, many factors affect the prices of stocks. Over the long haul, high interest rates or inflation can erode value. In addition, many stocks will respond to business trends or news about government regulation. In the short term, stocks often move for no apparent reason—sometimes out of sympathy for other stocks responding to their own news, and sometimes carried along by the broader market.

Yes, stocks are risky. But when it comes to investing, risk and reward are tradeoffs. If you want higher returns, you usually need to take on more risk. Historically, stocks have rewarded investors willing to accept the risk, as the chart below shows.

STOCKS OUTPERFORM BONDS

Asset class	Average annual return	Standard deviation
SMALL COMPANY STOCKS	16.5%	32.3%
LARGE COMPANY STOCKS	11.8%	20.2%
LONG-TERM GOVERNMENT BONDS	6.1%	9.7%
TREASURY BILLS	3.6%	3.1%

Source: Ibbotson SBBI 2013 Classic Yearbook, Morningstar.

Since 1926, stocks of large companies have averaged annual returns of 11.8%. Small company stocks have performed even better, averaging returns of more than 16% a year. But note the standard deviation, which measures risk. The higher the number, the more volatile the investment's returns from year to year.

If you want to earn long-term returns of more than 6% on your investments, you'll need to own stocks. Just be aware that while the long-term trend points upward, nothing is a sure thing, and you'll have to stomach plenty of dips and dives along the way.

BONDS

When companies wish to borrow money without taking out a bank loan, they can issue bonds. For example, say a company needs $10 million to expand. Instead of taking out a loan, it can sell $10 million in bonds to investors. The company receives the money and commits to paying a prearranged interest rate—generally in semiannual payments—until the bond matures and the company repays the borrowed funds in full.

Bond prices are affected less by the issuer's operating results (sales, earnings, etc.) than by changes in perceived creditworthiness. Still, by far the largest driver of bond-price moves is interest rates. In general, bond prices tend to rise when interest rates fall and decline when interest rates rise.

Suppose a company issues a bond with a face value of $10,000 that pays interest of $500 a year and will mature in 10 years. The bond yields 5% ($500 dividend by the $10,000 face value). If the 10-year Treasury bond pays interest of 2%, then the new corporate bond pays a 3% premium to the Treasury bond. Because Treasury bonds are perceived to have no risk of default (the issuer failing to pay back the bond), Treasury bonds are are the standard by which most other bonds are measured.

Investors in the new bond could choose instead to buy Treasury bonds, and the corporate bond's yield suggests buyers are willing to accept an extra 3% as compensation for the default risk. (Experienced investors will recognize this as a simplified explanation, because the relationship between Treasury and corporate bond yields isn't that clean. But the theory is sound, and the trend strong.)

If the Treasury bond yield rises to 3%, investors still expect a yield premium of roughly 3% to take on the corporate bond's default risk. However, the bond pays a fixed dividend of $500, based on the face value of $10,000. In order for $500 in dividends to generate a 6% yield to accommodate investors, the bond's price would have to dip to about $8,300. Of course, if the benchmark yield falls, the corporate bond's current payment will seem more valuable by comparison, and the price will rise.

Investors can purchase bonds issued by corporations, the U.S. Treasury Department, other government agencies, or municipalities. Bonds in general carry less risk than stocks, but within the bond market, different types of bonds carry drastically different risks. The three rules of thumb below will help you assess the risks of bonds.

1. Long-term bonds, or those with maturities far in the future, tend to be more volatile, meaning they'll respond more sharply to changes in interest rates. Since bonds pay back the face value (also called par value) when they mature, they will revert back toward the face value as they near maturity. Bonds close to maturity won't move much even if the prevailing interest rate changes.

2. In most cases, the higher a bond's yield, the riskier it is. If ABC Corp. issues a 10-year bond paying 5% and DEF Corp. issues a 10-year bond paying 7%, the yields reflect how much reward investors expect in turn for taking on the bond's risk. Naturally, buyers will expect a higher yield from a riskier bond.

3. Agencies such as Moody's and Standard & Poor's publish credit ratings that reflect the default risk of a bond issuer. S&P's top rating is AAA, with AA and A ratings lower down on the ladder. Any bond rated BBB- or higher is considered investment grade, while bonds with lower ratings are called either high-yield or junk bonds. More yield, of course, implies more risk.

Investors can purchase both stocks and bonds, but researching individual companies takes time and expertise. Fortunately, there is another option.

MUTUAL FUNDS

Mutual funds combine the resources of many investors and purchase a selection of stocks, bonds, or other securities, often mixing different types of assets. Fund companies hire professional managers to make buy and sell decisions, and everyone who invests in the fund earns a similar return.

Passively managed funds, often called index funds, try to match the returns of an index. Indexes are baskets (or collections) of stocks or bonds designed to represent the performance of a slice of the financial market. The best known is the S&P 500 Index, which contains large-company stocks and aims to reflect the returns of the overall U.S. market for large-company stocks. Mutual funds may track indexes that contain small-company stocks, different types of bonds, and pretty much any other type of investment.

Actively managed funds, on the other hand, attempt to outperform their benchmark index, relying on the manager's skill at analyzing and trading stocks or bonds. A key benefit of mutual funds over choosing your own stocks and bonds to purchase is their reliance on an expert to make investment decisions. Of course, investors will pay a management fee to compensate that expert.

THE INVESTMENT DECISION

If you find investing a fascinating topic and relish diving into analysis and research, then individual stocks—and possibly some of the many other types of investments—may be right for you.

Hundreds of books have been written on this topic, but you should really put in the time to find the investments best for you. If you have found this book to be helpful so far, you should check out *Stock Market For Beginners*. Regardless of the investment decisions you make, by now you've learned that nobody else will work as hard to build your wealth as you will.

FINDING THE RIGHT FUNDS

If you decide to opt for index funds (i.e., mutual funds that attempt to track the movement of a particular stock or bond index), take the fund's fees into account. After all, if the fund's job is to approximate the return of a group of stocks or bonds that many other similar funds will own, then the fund with the lowest fees often makes the most sense. Vanguard is known for its low fees and claims its average expense ratio is 83% below the industry average.

While Vanguard funds tend to offer the lowest expense ratios, you should also consider historical performance and performance relative to other funds when making investment decisions. You can find a wealth of information at www.morningstar.com.

But investment analysis isn't for everyone. Unless you're willing to put in the time and effort, stick with mutual funds (preferably index funds). When selecting mutual funds, consider the following features:

- Morningstar's star rating. Five stars is the best.
- Expense ratio (management fee).
- Historical performance.
- Performance versus the category average.
- Manager's tenure—experience is the best teacher.

The kind of mutual fund you should invest in depends on factors ranging from your age to your level of comfort with risk. For a good estimate, subtracting your age from 110 can give you a baseline for your stock exposure, with the rest in bonds. For example, a 50-year-old would subtract 50 from 110 and establish a baseline of 60% stocks, with the remaining 40% in bonds. From that baseline, you can adjust the weightings. Factors that would suggest raising the allocation to stocks include high wealth and good health. On the other hand, investors who either expect to need cash soon or are uncomfortable taking on risk should probably overweight the bond portion of the portfolio.

INVESTING FOR RETIREMENT

Do you know anyone who retired without enough money and had to scale his lifestyle down as he aged? That kind of devolution is painful to watch, and worse to experience. So don't travel that road.

The holy grail of investment milestones is retirement. Everything else—even college funding—must be subordinate to the idea of building a nest egg for retirement. Whenever possible, you should keep growing your retirement portfolio. Throughout your debt payoff and throughout life's various stages, an expanding retirement account can bring much peace of mind.

What beats a growing retirement portfolio? Try one that's protected from tax liability. Good money managers take advantage of federal tax breaks whenever possible. With that in mind, you should ensure that you partake of at least one of the following retirement plans.

401(K)

As companies shifted from traditional pensions to plans that put the majority of the funding burden back on the employee, 401(k) plans have become increasingly popular over the last 30 years. The 401(k) plan allows workers to set aside some of their paycheck before taxes, where it can grow in an account without the taxman's interference. Sure, you'll pay taxes when you withdraw the money—generally not until you reach retirement age—at which point you will have presumably graduated to a lower tax bracket.

A 401(k) differs from a pension plan in several ways:

- You control the investment. Each plan provides workers a variety of investment options, with an average of 19 funds per plan. The quality of those options varies greatly, with some offering a broad selection of mutual funds, while others limit employees to a few possibilities. Some plans feature publicly traded mutual funds you can research, and about two-thirds of plans offer customized "target-date" funds consisting of blends of stocks and bonds that become more conservative as you near retirement age; some *only* offer such funds.

- Most employers at least partially match employee contributions, according to the Plan Sponsor Council of America. The PSCA says that in 2012, participants in 401(k) plans contributed an average of 6.8% of their salaries to the plans, with companies averaging 4.5% contributions. That 4.5% includes profit-sharing contributions. Here's how the match usually works: Suppose Jimmy's employer matches 50% of his contributions, up to 6% of his salary. That means that if he contributes 6% of his $50,000 salary ($3,000), the company will add an extra $1,500 to the account every year. If Jimmy only contributes 3% of his salary ($1,500), the company contribution falls to $750.

- You may have the option to borrow from the plans (89% allow it), though you shouldn't do it. Whenever you take money out of an investment account, you lose some of the benefit of compounding. If you leave or lose the job, you'll probably have to pay the loan off immediately.

- You can take money out early if you like—at the cost of a 10% penalty on top of the tax liability. Most plans allow penalty-free withdrawals for employees facing financial hardships, but the requirements are fairly stiff. "I need the money to pay off my credit card" won't cut it.

- While the plans aren't portable, the money is. When you leave the company, you can transfer your assets to your new employer's 401(k) plan or another tax-deferred retirement account without losing its tax protection. This transfer is called a rollover.
- The Internal Revenue Service limits how much you can contribute to these plans. In 2013, the maximum was $17,500, though employees age 50 or older can kick in another $5,500.

401(k) Dos and Don'ts

- Do participate in your employer's 401(k) plan if it includes a company match. Contribute at least enough to capture all of the company's contribution. Even if you're trying to pay off debt, don't turn down free money. Think of it as a raise that doesn't require you to do any extra work.
- Don't borrow from your 401(k). A couple thousand borrowed now and repaid over time could cost you tens of thousands in lost value many years from now when you retire.
- Do research the investment options before you make a selection. Most employees should select a mix of stock and bond funds.
- Don't invest more than 10% of your own contributions in company stock, even if that stock is one of the investment options. Your job itself is already tied to the health of the company. Investing heavily in your company's stock may be riskier than it seems.

INDIVIDUAL RETIREMENT ARRANGEMENT (IRA)

These accounts provide similar tax protections as the 401(k) plan, but they don't operate the same way. You must open your own IRA—usually through a brokerage, bank, or mutual-fund company—and direct your own investment activity.

The tax deferral for a traditional IRA allows investors to deduct deposits of up to $5,500 ($6,500 for investors 50 or older). Anyone with taxable income or married to someone with taxable income can contribute to an IRA. However, if you currently own a 401(k) plan, your contributions will not be tax deductible. If you exceed income limitations, you lose the ability to deduct contributions from your taxes. Visit IRS.gov for details.

Like 401(k) plans, IRAs allow for hardship distributions, but you can't borrow from an IRA. One variant of the IRA, called the Coverdell Education Savings Account (formerly called the education IRA), allows contributions on behalf of children who do not have earned income. These make excellent vehicles for college savings.

IRA Dos and Don'ts

- Don't contribute more than the deductible limit unless you've exhausted all of your other tax-deferred options, such as maxing out your 401(k) contribution.
- Do start taking withdrawals from your IRA once you turn 70 1/2 years old, or you'll pay a penalty.
- Don't take money out of your IRA until you turn 59 1/2 years old, or you'll pay a penalty.
- Do roll over 401(k) plans into an IRA when you leave the company. Rollover contributions are exempted from the annual limit.

ROTH IRAS AND 401(K) PLANS

While traditional IRAs and 401(k) plans allow you to make tax-deductible contributions and defer taxation until you start withdrawing funds from the account, the IRS allows another option. Roth IRAs are funded with after-tax dollars, meaning you can't deduct the contribution.

However, the balance in a Roth IRA grows tax-free, and you can withdraw it without paying any taxes as long as you follow the IRS's rules. Investors under age 59 1/2 will pay the 10% tax penalty for most withdrawals from Roth IRAs, but unlike the case with traditional IRAs, investors are not required to start taking money out at age 70 1/2.

Roth 401(k) plans operate in much the same way as traditional plans, except that the contributions are made after tax and the withdrawals are tax-free. Not all employers offer a Roth option for their 401(k) plan, so talk to your human-resources department before you get too excited.

While Roth IRAs and 401(k) plans cost more up front because of the taxable contributions, the longer you have before retirement, the more sense they make relative to the traditional versions. As a rule of thumb, if you're more than 20 years away from retirement, you should probably opt for the Roth version of either retirement plan if you can. If you have the cash to pay the taxes up front and still max out your annual contribution, the Roth version may prove the better option even if you're nearing retirement age.

CHAPTER 8

THE BIGGEST DEALS

"The strength of a nation derives from
the integrity of the home."

—Confucius

NO DISCUSSION OF INVESTMENTS would be complete without
a little time spent on the largest investments most individuals will ever
make: buying a home, and paying for college. Both of these big expenses
require special treatment because they are unique among investments.

In October 2013, the median home in the U.S. sold for $199,500—a lot
of money for most people. According to the College Board, a "moderate"
budget for the 2012–2013 academic year at a four-year college averaged
$22,261 for an in-state student (versus $43,289 for a private college).
Four years of that kind of expense can put a dent in any budget.

HOME SWEET HOME

Over long periods of time, real estate probably won't deliver the returns
you could generate from stocks, but homes serve as more than an
investment.

While you can sell your stocks to buy food, you can't eat them. Apart
from the value of the company they represent, and the potential for earnings over time, stocks have no inherent use or value. A house, on the other
hand, provides value simply because you can live in it without paying

rent to someone else. This benefit comes in addition to the investment value. Since 1975, housing has appreciated in value at an average of 4.5% per year—less than half of the long-run return of stocks. When you figure in the cost of the apartment you don't have to rent, the returns get a lot closer.

So, should you buy a home, or should you rent? Both choices offer financial advantages. But for most people, the decision to buy a home goes far beyond the question of whether or not you can afford it. Here's how owning and renting stack up, based on seven key criteria:

1. **Time:** Homeowners will spend more time taking care of their place than will renters. Mowing lawns, shoveling snow, and fixing leaky faucets all add up. *Advantage:* Renting

2. **Cost to buy:** These days, lenders insist on down payments, with the preference being nearly 20%. Buyers with good credit can put less down, but for most people, if you don't have several thousand dollars saved up, you can't buy a house. Renters may have to pay a security deposit and the first and last month's rent before moving in, but not always. *Advantage:* Renting

3. **Cost to live:** Renters don't pay for taxes, maintenance, and in some cases even utilities. Owners, on the other hand, have to replace appliances, fix fences, and repave driveways. If you own a home, your budget should contain a category for home repairs and upkeep. If you don't pay someone else to do the jobs, refer back to the bullet point about time. Homeowners can deduct mortgage interest from their taxes, though the savings probably won't offset maintenance costs. *Advantage:* Renting

4. **Value:** According to the National Association of Realtors, the median rent for a three-bedroom apartment in the U.S. is $1,110, based on Fair Market Rent standards. In much of the country, you can purchase a three-bedroom home—which tends to have more

square footage than an apartment—for $1,000 a month or less. Factor in the home's price appreciation, and the value proposition is clear. *Advantage:* Owning

5. **Flexibility to move:** Owners never know how long it will take to sell their home, and real-estate agents generally charge 6% to 7% commissions. However, renters usually sign leases that require them to stay in the apartment for a specific period of time. If you need to move before that time expires, you may have to pay a fee, but at least you won't get stuck paying for a house you don't live in. *Advantage:* Renting

6. **Flexibility to live:** Most apartments limit what tenants can do to the property, such as painting the walls or adding closets. Homeowners can remodel or add on if they wish. *Advantage:* Owning

7. **Independence:** Landlords can kick you out at the end of the lease for any reason. When you own a home, you can generally hold onto it as long as you keep current on the mortgage. *Advantage:* Owning

So which makes the most sense? Only you can determine that, as much depends on your needs and on which factors in the housing decision are most important to you. Neither owning nor renting is always superior to the other.

That said, purchasing a home is certainly a more complicated endeavor than renting, particularly from a financial standpoint. To start with, unless you're paying cash, you'll need a mortgage. You already know how to account for the costs in your budget, and you understand the qualities bankers seek. But before you take the leap to a mortgage, make sure you're prepared to do the following five things:

1. Look far ahead.

Because houses are so expensive, people often need decades to pay for them. Most traditional (fixed-rate) mortgages carry a 30-year term and generate massive interest costs. According to the mortgage loan calculator at Bankrate.com, if you take out a $200,000 loan at 4.5% with a 30-year term, your monthly payment for principal and interest is $1,103.

If you make all 360 payments, you'll pay off the $200,000 loan, but you'll also make $165,000 in interest payments. Not only that, but interest is front-loaded. During the first decade you'll pay $82,000 in interest, versus just $40,000 of the principal. Yuck.

2. Go shorter when it matters.

The picture looks better for a 15-year mortgage than it does for one that lasts 30 years. The same $200,000 loan carries a payment of $1,530—39% higher than the payment on a 30-year loan. However, if you make all the payments for 15 years, you'll spend about $75,000 on interest, which is less than you'd pay during just the first 10 years of a 30-year loan. The numbers make your choice plain.

If at all possible, go with a 15-year or 20-year mortgage rather than a 30-year. To further limit your interest costs, try paying more than the monthly payment and applying any surplus directly to the principal.

3. Adjust at your own risk.

If you prefer, you can take out an adjustable-rate mortgage (ARM). These mortgages lock in an interest rate for a few years, then adjust based on the prevailing rate going forward. This means your payment could go up or down sharply, depending on the overall direction of interest rates. ARMs tend to offer low interest rates and payments during the early years of the loan, which often appeal to buyers.

ARMs make some sense if either you're confident interest rates will fall going forward or you know you're going to sell the house before the rate adjusts. Before you jump on board, consider how tough it is to predict the future. You don't know what interest rates will do, and you could probably think of a dozen reasons why you might not sell your house in two years. ARMs are riskier than they look. Just ask the people who lost their homes to foreclosure after their rates jumped before the housing crisis.

FOUR TIPS TO MAKE THE HOME-BUYING PROCESS EASIER

Buying a home can intimidate even experienced money managers. Here are four simple steps to help you deal with the stress:

1. Find a real estate agent you trust, and who has plenty of experience. Ask all the questions you want. If the agent won't provide the answers, you have the wrong agent.

2. Be picky about your lender. Look at the rates, particularly the APR (annual percentage rate, including fees). Look at the fees. And look very, very carefully at the property before you buy. The day after the loan closes is a bad time to realize you should have held out for more square footage, or that the foundation is unsteady.

3. Don't buy more than you can afford. Remember, no real estate agent or mortgage lender has a clue what you can afford. Run any purchase through your budget, using conservative assumptions regarding costs, before you make a move. If you have any doubts about whether you can afford the house, go with a less-expensive home.

4. Pay for a home inspector. The inspector will find problems; every home has them. But the more you know about the house, the more effectively you can negotiate the price.

4. Bring some cash to the table.

Your lender will expect a down payment on the house (preferably 20% of the home's value). You'll also need to pay your real-estate agent's commission (generally 6% to 7%), as well as closing costs on the loan. Closing costs include fees for appraisals, title work, document preparation, and other charges levied by the lender.

Zillow.com estimates closing costs at 2% to 5% of the purchase price of the home, but you can usually keep the number toward the low end if you shop around. When you compare mortgage-loan offers, don't be fooled by the confusing names of the fees charged. The number you want is the total amount of fees charged for the loan. You can either pay the fees up front or fold them into the loan itself. However, financing a $350 appraisal over 15 years seems foolish, so pay the fees in cash if you can.

5. Plan for a higher payment.

The loan payments listed in the first bullet point only cover the principal (loan value) and interest on that principal. Homeowners will take on several other costs that vary depending on the price and location of the home. Make sure you budget for property taxes and homeowners insurance. Your real-estate agent can provide you with historical tax bills for a home you're considering, and your insurance agent can price a homeowners policy.

If you bring less than 20% of the home's value as a down payment, you'll have to pay private mortgage insurance (PMI), which protects the lender in the case that you default. Most mortgage lenders will bundle taxes, insurance, and PMI into your monthly mortgage payment. Once you've paid off enough of the principal that you owe less than 80% of the value of the home, you no longer have to pay the PMI. Of course, mortgage lenders may not remind you of this promptly, so keep track of the loan's progress yourself and remind *them* when you cross the threshold.

THE LEARNING CURVE

College qualifies as an investment because it can increase a student's long-term earning power, thus making their future income stream more valuable. In 2008, adults with bachelor's degrees averaged annual salaries $22,000 higher than those with just a high school diploma. Whether a particular college is a good investment depends on how well you plan.

Total college costs include a variety of expenses:

- Tuition covers the cost of instruction.
- Fees include costs for parking, registration, student activities, insurance, and a host of other possibilities that vary from school to school.
- Housing and meals combine to eat up $9,000 to $11,000.
- The cost for books and school supplies averages about $1,200.
- Personal and transportation expenses average $2,500 to $3,200.

Shrewd students and parents can reduce these costs by purchasing used books, as well as by cutting back on entertainment and other personal expenditures, but the bulk of these costs cannot be reduced.

Most students receive some form of financial aid. About 53% of aid comes in the form of grants and scholarships students don't have to repay, with another 10% coming from tax credits, deductions, and work-study programs. The remainder represents federal loans.

To maximize aid, students and parents should get started early. Here are some recommendations:

Invest, invest, invest. In addition to the investment options discussed in Chapter 7, parents may want to set up a 529 plan. Nearly every state offers at least one of these plans, which allow parents to invest money in a tax-preferred account. Parents can contribute to most plans regardless of their income and invest far more than the IRS allows for an IRA. The drawback? You can only use the funds for educational purposes. Compare the plans at Savingforcollege.com, as they vary greatly in quality and flexibility. In most cases, you can live in one state, invest in another state's plan, then send your kid to college in a third state.

Search for scholarships. Don't wait until the junior or senior year. Scour scholarship databases and apply for everything that might apply. While academic excellence drives most scholarship selections, many use other criteria, and even students without the best grade-point averages may win scholarships.

File the FAFSA. Every student should file the Free Application for Federal Student Aid (FAFSA) and submit it to the state where she intends to go to school. Submit as early as the state allows, because some financial aid goes to the first students who request it. Not surprisingly, more aid tends to flow to families with the least money.

Get a job. Students can apply for federally funded work-study jobs on campus. The amount of money available varies based on when you apply, your level of financial need, and how much funding your school has set aside for them.

Cultivate reasonable expectations. Your child may have their heart set on a name-brand college or university. But if you can't afford it, you can't afford it. Millions of Americans earn high-quality degrees at state schools and still pursue lucrative careers.

Don't rule out the top schools. While private schools cost more than state schools, some boast rich endowments and can offer far more aid than public universities. Go ahead and pursue the high-end colleges if your student has the grades to get in. You might be surprised. Just remember the previous bullet point and don't set your heart on a specific school in case it proves out of reach.

Of course, both students and parents can take advantage of federal loan programs—some of which don't require payment until after graduation. However, you should always avoid taking loans if you can. If you need to borrow more than $50,000 (many people would cap that at $20,000) for an undergraduate education, you've probably paid too much. If you do decide to borrow, estimate the loan-payoff costs and let your budget tell you how much you can afford.

CHAPTER 9

KEEPING AND PROTECTING IT

EVERYONE ENJOYS MAKING MONEY. When you do a job and earn a buck, you know where it came from. And if you maintain a budget, you also know where it will go. Investing also appeals to people. A little today turning into a lot tomorrow? Who wouldn't want to see that?

The earning, spending, and investing parts of personal finance get the best headlines. They're interesting. Exciting. Sexy, even; we've all seen Hollywood movies that make Wall Street investors look like rock stars. But in between the earning and the spending (and especially between the spending and the investing) what happens to that money? You've got to find somewhere to keep it safe, some way to access it easily without taking too many risks.

How do you choose and use a bank? What kind of insurance should you buy? How can you limit your tax burden? These are important questions, but admittedly not very enticing. On campus, banks, insurance, and taxes are the nerds who don't get the girls. But as the last generation taught us, nerds often assume positions of importance and respect when they grow up. The true money manager neglects them at his peril, because they make it possible to do the fun stuff. Without any further ado, it's time to talk banks, insurance, and taxes.

WHERE THE MONEY IS

You've probably heard some version of the old joke: What do you give the man who has everything? Somewhere to keep it.

You likely don't have everything, but you probably do have a little money, and you should give some thought about where you keep it. Most Americans know these basics:

- A checking account allows you to send payments to your creditors without risking cash in the mail.

- A savings account simply holds your money, paying you very little interest for the privilege. You should have one, but unless you need a place to park funds for a very short time, you probably won't use it much.

- Bank savings and checking accounts are insured for up to $250,000 apiece by the Federal Deposit Insurance Corporation against a bank failure. (The FDIC was instituted to protect banks and consumers alike during the Great Depression, when many banks failed due to the stock market crash, and subsequently, many individuals lost their life's savings.)

- A money market fund is a step above a savings account, but not a big step. These invest in short-term, high-quality debt, providing a safe place to invest cash. Historically, they've tended to pay higher yields than interest rates paid by savings accounts, though in an environment of extremely low interest rates (such as that seen from 2009 through 2013) neither money markets nor savings accounts paid much.

- Debit cards allow you to deposit or withdraw money at ATMs, and to make purchases without carrying cash, drawing the funds directly from your checking account. However, since ATMs charge fees and wise money managers prefer not to pay fees, you should limit your use of ATMs unless your bank covers the costs.

- Banks provide customers with loans to purchase cars and other items, and many also make mortgage and home-equity loans.

Just about every bank does a fine job of providing these services, so how do you select which one to use? Visit websites, make some calls, and compare them based on these four criteria:

1. **Fees.** Consider the services you currently demand from your bank, then see what other banks charge for those services. Look for banks that don't charge monthly fees on accounts, and ones that reimburse ATM fees.

2. **Interest rates.** How much interest does the bank pay on its savings accounts? Does the bank offer an interest-paying checking account that doesn't charge a fee?

3. **Special services.** Some banks provide more services than others. If you use your bank for something more than a place to keep your cash, find out whether other banks do the same thing better or cheaper.

4. **Customer service.** You can tell a lot about how a bank views customer service by calling and by visiting its website. If you aren't satisfied with your current bank's service, see if you can find something better.

Notice that location wasn't among the criteria. If you need to visit a bank branch frequently, then limit your search to firms with offices near your home or workplace. However, if you're comfortable banking online, you'll enjoy more and better choices.

More than half of U.S. adults bank online and 32% transact business on mobile phones. Online banking doesn't change how you use your money; it only changes how you interact with your bank. Of course, with traditional banks letting customers view accounts and pay bills online, the line between online and brick-and-mortar banks has blurred.

FIVE FACTS ABOUT ONLINE BANKS

1. Better rates: Helped by lower operating costs (no brick-and-mortar branches), in early 2013 online banks averaged interest rates six times higher than the national average, according to MoneyRates.com.

2. Lower fees: Online banks are twice as likely as traditional banks to offer free checking, and they tend to set lower limits on account balances before assessing a maintenance fee.

3. Solid security: While some consumers worry about their information being stolen, even traditional banks keep financial records in data centers, so the risks are no higher with online banks.

4. Different types of deposits: Online banks let customers mail checks in, but most also allow customers to photograph and scan their checks, then deposit them online.

5. ATM networks: Many online banks either negotiate with ATM networks to cut fees or reimburse the fees for their customers.

Source: MoneyRates.com

INSURANCE TO EMBRACE OR AVOID

Insurance serves one purpose: in exchange for you paying a fee (called a premium), it will compensate you or someone you owe in the event that something bad happens. This suggests that you should buy insurance if:

- The potential financial loss is too high for you to bear alone.
- The premiums seem reasonable relative to the size of that loss.
- You will, in fact, be held liable for damages if a negative event occurs.

With those three facts in mind, you can divide insurance into two informal categories: the good stuff and the bad stuff.

THE GOOD STUFF

Automobile insurance. This isn't just good; it's required by law in most states. A car is the deadliest weapon most people will ever own, as evidenced by the people who died in auto accidents in 2011, according to the National Highway Traffic Safety Administration. Don't just purchase the minimum coverage required. Bump your liability coverage up to $1 million. The difference in the premium between $100,000 and $1 million isn't that big, and if someone sues you, that $100,000 can disappear quickly.

Liability coverage pays for damage to other people or property. Collision coverage pays for damage to your car. Typical policies also help pay for medical expenses for you and your passengers, and for damages caused by drivers with no insurance. All but collision are no-brainers. Collision coverage tends to be expensive, and if you still owe money on the car, your lender probably requires it. If you own the car outright, you probably don't need the coverage if you have enough cash to repair or replace the car.

Health insurance. Most workers obtain coverage through their employers. But with health-reform legislation just getting off the ground, the health-insurance picture is cloudy. Talk to your human resources director for guidance. Grouped in here are dental and vision coverage. The quality of these policies can vary, so check the size of the provider network and the policy benefits. You may be better off paying retail price for glasses at a nationwide optical chain than purchasing subpar vision insurance.

Long-term disability insurance. Many people forget about this one, but they shouldn't. Social Security Administration statistics suggest that three of every 10 workers will eventually become disabled and unable to work before they reach retirement age. Nearly 50% of all mortgage foreclosures are caused by disability, versus just 2% by death. If your employer provides disability coverage, take advantage of it. If you need to get it yourself, don't hesitate. Pay a low premium to avoid a high risk.

Homeowners/renters insurance. Mortgage companies will require this, but many renters don't bother with it, and it can be a potentially dangerous omission. You might think, "I've got nothing worth stealing." But the true value in renters insurance lies in the liability protection. If someone slips in your bathroom or chokes on a chicken bone in your dining room, you may be liable for damages if your visitor sues. Don't go cheap here. Get the coverage.

Life insurance. This one makes the "good stuff" list because the coverage has value. However, not everyone needs it. If you have children or nonworking spouses who depend on you for support, then buy life insurance to protect them in the event that you die. Married couples without children may still want insurance, and they'll pay less if they purchase it early in life. Not surprisingly, products that pay a death benefit tend to become more expensive as you age. With rare exceptions, single adults and children do not need life insurance.

Even if life insurance makes sense for you, don't go overboard. Select a simple term life policy. In exchange for a fixed premium over a fixed time, the company agrees to pay a fixed death benefit. Companies will try to sell you whole life or universal life or variable life or whatever the latest name is. Insurers make the most money by selling policies that combine the death benefit with an investment. However, insurance companies tend to invest conservatively and charge high fees. Instead of paying for these policies, just buy term insurance—which is much cheaper—and handle the investing yourself. Some experts suggest purchasing coverage equal to five years of your take-home pay, but play it safe and double that. The extra coverage shouldn't boost the premium too much, and your family deserves it.

THE BAD STUFF

Cancer insurance. If you have life insurance and good health insurance, you don't need the extra coverage, or the extra premium.

Mortgage life insurance. This coverage will pay your mortgage if you die. In effect, you're protecting a mortgage-lending company at your expense. Better to make sure you have enough term life insurance so your beneficiaries can pay off the mortgage.

Credit life insurance. A lot like mortgage life insurance, except that your beneficiaries may not even be liable for the credit-card bill.

Accidental death insurance. Once again, this coverage duplicates your more comprehensive life insurance, and these policies won't pay out if your family can't prove the accident directly caused your death.

Flight insurance. Another coverage duplication, not to mention a premium way too high given the tiny chance that you'll die in a plane crash.

Insurance for rental cars. Take care of this by making sure your own auto insurance covers you when you drive rental cars. Most companies provide this coverage for far less than the rental company would charge. Many credit cards also provide this coverage as a member benefit.

Flood insurance. Unless you live in an area that floods frequently, you probably don't need this expensive coverage.

TACKLING TAXES

There's a reason why almost 60% of Americans will pay a professional to do their taxes this year and another 30% will use tax software to handle the job: complexity. Tax law has undergone major changes in almost every year over the past half-century, and in 2011 the IRS commissioner said that since 2000, there have been about 3,500 changes in the law. Come tax time, you'll face an important decision. Will you do your own taxes or pay someone else to do them?

FIVE TAX DEDUCTIONS MANY PEOPLE MISS

In 2012, 92 million taxpayers claimed the standard deduction based on their filing status (single, married, head of household, etc.) while 45 million itemized. Nobody knows how many people cost themselves money by taking the simple route, but nearly everybody ends up paying taxes, and only a fool turns down the chance to reduce their bill. With that in mind, here are five deductions you don't want to forget:

1. State sales taxes. Taxpayers can choose whether to deduct state sales taxes or state income taxes. Many choose income taxes and don't bother looking at sales taxes. But if you made some big-ticket purchases like cars or other vehicles, the sales-tax deduction might save you more money. (Make sure to always check the current status of federal and state tax laws before making these kinds of decisions.)

2. Student loan interest paid by parents. If parents pay back loans taken out in the student's name, the IRS acts as if the child received the money from the parents and paid the loans on their own. In such cases, the student can deduct the interest.

If you decide to do the job yourself, spring for some software. The days of pencil and paper have long passed, and software will reduce your chances of making mistakes.

If you seek outside help, don't go cheap. A simple return should cost $50 to $100, and if you hire someone who will give you personal attention, don't be afraid to pay near the top end.

An IRS official once told *Kiplinger's Personal Finance* that millions of taxpayers overpaid their taxes by missing out on deductions. A professional tax preparer should spot some of those missed deductions.

3. Noncash charitable donations. You can deduct many of the out-of-pocket costs you incur while helping a charitable organization. For instance, if you donate food or cook for your church's free-meals program, you can deduct the cost of the food, though not the value of your time. The IRS also allows a deduction for mileage on your auto.

4. Job-search costs. You can only deduct these costs if your miscellaneous expenses (which also include employee expenses not reimbursed by the company, union dues, and work-related travel) top 2% of your gross income. But young people just starting out and those who spent some time unemployed might easily have racked enough expenses to qualify for the deduction.

5. Refinancing points. When you refinance your mortgage, you have the option to pay 1% of the balance (a point) to reduce the interest rate, which lowers your monthly payment. If you purchased one or more points, you can deduct them on your taxes over the life of the loan.

Tax software won't know whether you're entitled to a deduction, but programs like TurboTax and TaxCut will point out the deductions and explain them so you can make the determination yourself.

Before you decide whether to tackle your own taxes, ask yourself two questions:

- Are you scared of numbers? Software will help you fill out the forms and do the math, but you must perform your own recordkeeping. If paperwork bores or intimidates you, you're probably not a good bet for doing your own taxes.
- Can you spare the time? In 2012 the IRS estimated that the average taxpayer spent 22 hours preparing 2011 tax returns, and 32 hours for those who filed schedules for businesses or rental properties. However, like most averages, this number is skewed by a relatively small number of people who spend hundreds of hours on their taxes. Still, if you plan to do your own taxes, take the time to do them right.

Should you do your own taxes? That's another one of those issues that puts the personal in finance. Just remember this last piece of advice. If you have doubt, hire it out.

THE REST OF THE STORY

The headline above promises that there's more to the story. And there is, but not in this book. Nobody can tell the rest of your story except you.

Your journey has just begun.

Remember that when you decide to become a money manager, the job remains yours for as long as you keep doing the work. Nobody can fire you except yourself, so hold steady and never take your eyes off your financial goals.

SUGGESTED READING

Stock Market for Beginners by Callisto Media.

The Little Book of Living Frugal by Dr. Charlotte Gorman.

365 Ways to Live Cheap! by Trent Hamm.

Home Finances for Couples by Leo Ostapiv.

Money and Marriage by Maya Davis.

Common Sense On Mutual Funds by John Bogle.

One Up On Wall Street: How to Use What You Already Know to Make Money in the Market by Peter Lynch.

The Neatest Little Guide to Stock Market Investing by Jason Kelly.

The Bond Book: Everything Investors Need to Know About Treasuries, Municipals, GNMAs, Corporates, Zeros, Bond Funds, Money Market Funds, and More by Annette Thau.

The Home Mortgage Book: Insider Information Your Banker & Broker Don't Want You to Know by Dale Mayer.

Paying For College Without Going Broke by Kalman Chany.

ADDITIONAL RESOURCES

Automobiles: www.edmunds.com, www.kbb.com.

Coupons: www.couponcabin.com, www.retailmenot.com.

Budgeting: www.daveramsey.com, budgeting calculator at www.bankrate.com.

Shopping for used goods: www.ebay.com, www.craigslist.com.

Savings calculator: cgi.money.cnn.com/tools/savingscalc/
savingscalc.html.

Auto loan calculator: www.bankrate.com/calculators/auto/
auto-loan-calculator.aspx.

Student loan repayment: www.studentaid.ed.gov.

Household debt statistics: www.federalreserve.gov/econresdata
/default.htm.

Business loans: www.sba.gov.

College funding: www.studentaid.ed.gov.

Loan calculators: www.bankrate.com.

Free credit reports: www.annualcreditreport.com.

Credit scores: www.myfico.com.

Investment research: www.morningstar.com (mutual funds), finance.
yahoo.com, and money.msn.com/investing/ (company news for stock
and bond analysis).

401(k) plans: www.psca.org/55th-annual-survey-highlights.

Individual retirement arrangements (IRAs): www.irs.gov.

Mortgage calculators: www.bankrate.com.

College funding: www.studentaid.ed.gov, www.fafsa.ed.gov,
bigfuture.collegeboard.org/college-search, www.savingforcollege.com.

College search based on estimated net cost: bigfuture.collegeboard.org/
college-search

BIBLIOGRAPHY

"Moebs: Overdraft Revenue Increases Resulting from Higher Fees," *Credit Union Times*. September 10, 2013. www.cutimes.com/2013/09/10/moebs-overdraft-revenue-increases-resulting-from-h

"6 Things You Must Know About Tech Warranties," *Kiplinger*. December 2013. www.kiplinger.com/article/spending/T050-C000-S002-6-things-you-must-know-about-tech-warranties.html

"How You Can Save Hundreds with Underutilized Credit Card Perks," *Forbes*. Aug. 23, 2012. www.forbes.com/sites/moneybuilder/2012/08/23/how-you-can-save-hundreds-with-underutilized-credit-card-perks

"Three Myths about What Customers Want," *Harvard Business Review*. May 23, 2012. blogs.hbr.org/2012/05/three-myths-about-customer-eng

"The Cost of Marriage and Divorce," CNBC. May 7, 2012. www.cnbc.com/id/46806960

"Cash vs. Credit Mindset," *Chicago Tribune*. December 15, 2011. articles.chicagotribune.com/2011-12-15/news/sc-cons-1215-karpspend-20111210_1_credit-cards-card-balances-debit-cards

Auto Calculator, Bankrate. Accessed November 2013. www.bankrate.com/calculators/auto/auto-loan-calculator.aspx

Mortgage Calculator, Bankrate. Accessed November 2013. www.bankrate.com/calculators/mortgages/mortgage-calculator.aspx

"Average Cost to Raise a Kid: $241,080," CNN Money. August 14, 2013. money.cnn.com/2013/08/14/pf/cost-children

"Credit Card Statistics, Industry Facts, Debt Statistics," CreditCards.com. Accessed November 2013. www.creditcards.com/credit-card-news/credit-card-industry-facts-personal-debt-statistics-1276.php

"Report: Average Price of New Car Hits Record in August," *USA Today*. September 5, 2013. www.usatoday.com/story/money/cars/2013/09/04/record-price-new-car-august/2761341

"Divorce Study: Financial Arguments Early In Relationship May Predict Divorce," *Huffington Post*. November 28, 2013. www.huffingtonpost.com/2013/07/12/divorce-study_n_3587811.html

"Average Age of U.S. Car, Light Truck on Road Hits Record 11.4 Years, Polk Says," *Automotive News*. August 6, 2013. www.autonews.com/article/20130806/RETAIL/130809922/#axzz2lgUBNwEL

New-Car Prices, *Motor Trend*. Accessed November 2013. www.motortrend.com/new_cars/99/30_40/pricing

"U.S. Apartment Vacancy Rate Flat in Second Quarter, but Rents Rise," *Reuters*, July 8, 2013. www.reuters.com/article/2013/07/09/us-usproperty-apartments-idUSBRE96803X20130709

Economic Data, Federal Reserve. Accessed November 2013. www.federalreserve.gov/econresdata/default.htm

INDEX